D0527876

jams and
preserves

03588403

EAST SUSSEX
COUNTY LIBRARY

03588403

Askews	Aug-2010
641.852	£4.99
2921675	HASM.

LEW 6fu

jams and preserves

MURDOCH BOOKS

contents

making jams and preserves

Imagine eating delectable freshly poached peaches and fresh cherry jam in the middle of winter, or dollops of rich, fruity chutneys with the barbecue in the height of summer. With no previous skills required, preserving is a culinary adventure that can be both satisfying and rewarding.

For centuries, jams, preserves, chutneys and pickles have been made to ensure a regular food supply during colder and leaner times. They are best made during the peak of the season when the fruit and vegetables are plentiful and cheap. Obviously, the use of homegrown produce can save you lots of money, as can buying in bulk from produce markets.

WHICH FRUIT TO CHOOSE
When making jams, preserves, chutneys or pickles it is essential to use good-quality fruits and vegetables to get the best results. Always choose fruit that is firm and just ripe, and without any blemishes or bruises. Overripe fruit will lack the amount of pectin needed to set the preserve. If fruit is quite ripe, add about 10 per cent of underripe fruit to increase the pectin level to the amount needed to set the preserve.

SUGAR AND PECTIN
When making jams and jellies the balance of the acid in the fruit, the sugar and the pectin will all play a part in the final firmness

and flavour of the preserve. Sugar is not just used as a sweetener when making jams and jellies. It is also a preservative when used in a high concentration, inhibiting the development and growth of micro-organisms. To reach a high enough concentration, 250 g (9oz/1 cup) sugar must be used per 250 g (9 oz/1 cup) fruit. In other words, the weight of the sugar should be the same as the weight of whatever type of fruit you are using. Sugar is also a setting agent and aids the setting process in jams and jellies that would not set without a commercial setting agent.

Pectin is found in the skin, flesh and seeds of fruits in varying degrees. It is particularly high in citrus pith and apple skin. Some fruits are quite low in pectin or have none at all and need the addition of pectin-containing fruit or juice, or commercial setting agents, to help them set.

The acid level of the fruit is also important, because it acts as a preservative and setting agent. Acid levels can be supplemented with lemon juice or by combining several fruits together in a recipe. A commercial setting agent is not always needed. If the preserve sets when tested it may not be necessary to add it at all. Successful jams and preserves require an even balance of pectin and acid.

TESTING FOR PECTIN
If you are in doubt as to how much pectin is in the fruit you want to use to make your jelly, place 2 teaspoons of methylated spirits in a small bowl and then gently add 1 teaspoon of the strained fruit mixture and stir gently. If there is enough pectin present to set the jelly, clots should form into one large lump. If they form

smaller lumps, the mixture will need to be reduced some more or you will need to add some lemon juice. If it is still not setting, you may need to use a commercial setting agent.

SUGAR

You will notice that all our sweet preserve recipes call for warmed sugar. While warming the sugar before adding it to the pan is not absolutely imperative in a recipe and won't affect the final outcome, it does speed up the dissolving process. The sugar dissolves more quickly and, being warm, will not reduce the temperature of the fruit mixture as much as if you had added cold sugar. To warm sugar, spread it in an even layer in a deep-sided baking dish and put it in a slow oven 150°C (300°F/Gas 2) for 10–15 minutes, or until warmed through. Do not overheat the sugar, or it will start to lump together. To make sure, stir it once or twice while it is warming. To save time, you can warm the sugar while you are cooking the jam.

Do not add the sugar until the fruit has softened. If the sugar is added before the fruit is fully soft, it will stay firm. Regular granulated sugar is used in our jam, jelly and preserve recipes unless otherwise specified. Caster sugar is used in some recipes for quicker dissolving and better clarity. Brown sugar is used mostly in chutneys, pickles and relishes to enhance the flavours.

EQUIPMENT

Large heavy-based stainless steel or enamel pans are one of the most important pieces of equipment you can have when making jams and preserves. You can even buy special preserving pans if you intend to make large amounts.

Sugar thermometers are a very helpful gauge for temperatures. It is crucial, when bottling and sealing your preserve, that the temperature remains at or above 85°C (185°F). This prevents the growth of potentially harmful bacteria. If you don't have a sugar thermometer, make sure you seal your preserve in its jar as soon as it is ready. You can also use your thermometer to test whether your preserve has reached setting point. This generally occurs once the mixture has reached 104°C (220°F).

We haven't used the thermometer method much in this book, relying more on testing on a saucer with the wrinkle method. Jam funnels will come in handy and make filling jars a little easier without the jam dripping down the sides. Heatproof jugs are essential for pouring and measuring. A metal skimmer or metal spoon is ideal for removing scum from the surface of the jam or preserve. Ladles are often used to transfer cooked preserves to jars. Wooden spoons are needed for stirring, and, of course, a pastry brush to clean down the sides of the pan.

Muslin (cheesecloth) is used in this book both to drain liquids and to hold seeds and rind in a secure bundle. It can be bought at kitchenware or fabric stores. Alternatively, you can use a clean tea (dish) towel. When straining mixtures such as jellies, ensure the material is just damp so it won't absorb too much of the liquid.

Before starting to cook your jam or preserve, ensure your equipment has been carefully washed in hot, soapy water and the jars you intend to use are thoroughly clean. Always make sure you have enough clean jars ready for when you have a pan full of boiling jam ready to bottle. The best way to ensure that the jars are spotlessly clean is to preheat the oven to very slow 120°C (250°F/Gas ½). Thoroughly wash the jars and lids in hot, soapy water (or preferably in a dishwasher) and rinse well with hot water. Put the jars onto the baking trays and place them in the oven for 20 minutes, or until you are ready to use them. Dry them fully in the oven.

HOW IT ALL WORKS

Whether you are making jams, preserves, jellies, pickles, chutneys or relishes, the method is essentially the same. Obviously, sweet jams, preserves and jellies require a lot more sugar than the savoury pickles, chutneys and relishes. They are also self-setting in that the mixture thickens on cooling to an easily spreadable consistency.

JAMS

Try not to cook too much jam all in one quantity. Do not use more than 2 kg (4 lb) fruit in a recipe at a time. You also need to make sure that your pan is large enough. Ideally, the mixture should be no more than 5–6 cm (2–2½ inches) deep after the sugar has been added. Chutneys and pickles can be cooked in larger quantities, but remember the more mixture you have in the pan, the longer the cooking time. Jellies are generally cooked in smaller quantities.

Wash and dry the fruit well to remove any dirt. If you are using citrus fruits such as oranges or grapefruit, gently scrub the fruit with a soft bristle brush under warm running water to remove the wax coating. Remove any stalks from berries and cut away any damaged or bruised pieces of fruit (which you shouldn't have if you'd chosen your fruit carefully in the beginning!)

Cut up the fruit according to the recipe and place it into your pan to soften. Be aware that some recipes require the fruit to be soaked overnight. Reserved seeds and extra skin or fruit are used in many recipes in this book, particularly lemon pips and rind. These are wrapped in a square of muslin (cheesecloth) and can be soaked overnight with the fruit, and then cooked with the fruit, as in the case of marmalade, or simply added to the pan and cooked with the jam or preserve. For easy retrieval of the muslin (cheesecloth) bag, attach a long piece of string to the bag and tie it to the handle of the pan. The remaining ingredients are added according to each individual recipe.

Bring the mixture to the boil, then reduce the heat and simmer for the specified time until the fruit is tender, then add the required amount of sugar. Remove any scum or foam from the top of the jam or preserve all through the cooking process. The scum that forms on the top of the mixture is usually any impurities or dirt on the fruit or sugar. Stir over heat, without boiling, until all the sugar has dissolved. Brush the side of the pan with a pastry brush dipped in water, to dissolve any excess sugar crystals which can sometimes cause jams to crystallize towards the end of cooking. If the jam does crystallize, add 1–2 tablespoons of lemon juice and gently reheat. Be aware that this may change the taste slightly.

Once all the sugar has dissolved, boil the mixture rapidly for the required time. Stir the jam often while it is cooking to speed up the cooking process and ensure that it does not stick to the bottom of the pan.

After the specified cooking time is completed, or when the jam or preserve looks thick and syrupy, the mixture should fall from a wooden spoon heavily with 3 or 4 drops joining together as they drop. When this happens, it means that the jam or preserve has reached its setting point.

Cooking times vary greatly between recipes, depending on pan sizes, the fruit used, the time of year, if the fruit is in season, etc. Therefore, it is necessary to test for setting point, sometimes up to 10 minutes before the stated time, to make sure the jam or preserve is ready to be bottled. Do not rely entirely on the times stated. Remove the pan from the heat, place 1 teaspoon of the jam onto one of the cold plates and place it in the freezer for about 30 seconds, or until the jam has cooled to room temperature. Gently push through the jam with the tip of your finger. There should be a skin on top of the jam which should wrinkle. If it does wrinkle, it's ready. Ta da!! If not, return the mixture briefly to the heat and try again in a few minutes with the second plate.

Immediately spoon or pour the mixture into the warm, clean jars. Pulpier jams tend to have a thicker consistency and jams with large pieces of fruit will need a few minutes standing in the pan before bottling to allow the fruit to be evenly suspended in the mixture. Don't leave the jam or jelly for too long or it will start to set in the pan. If this does happen, you will need to start all over again. Take care when pouring the preserves into the jars as the mixture is extremely hot. Hold the jar in a tea towel and pour or spoon in the preserve, filling right to the top. If your jars have small openings it may be easier to pour the jam into a clean heatproof jug first and then into the jars. You can also use a jam funnel.

Occasionally, you will find you have air bubbles in the bottles. To remove them, use a thin clean skewer to help push mixture to the side and release the bubble to the surface. This technique can be used for all types of preserves. Alternatively, a gentle tap on a cloth on the bench will release some of the air bubbles. Seal the jars while the mixture is still hot. Turn the jars upside down for 2 minutes, then invert and leave to cool. This will ensure the fruit is evenly distributed and the lids are sterilized.

JELLIES

Choose fruits with a good pectin and acid balance for the best results. The fruit is cooked with or without water and then strained overnight in a damp jelly bag (these are available in good kitchenware stores) or damp muslin bag suspended over a stool. A wide bowl is placed underneath to catch liquid. Don't squeeze the jelly bag or the liquid and resulting jelly will turn cloudy. Youcan use the pectin test if necessary, but the recipes in this book give you the required amount of sugar for the fruit used. Add the sugar, stir until dissolved and then boil rapidly for the required time, following the same method for jams. Skimming off the scum is essential at this stage or it will make jelly cloudy later on. Before pouring into the clean, warm jars, allow any bubbles in the pan to subside. Pour the jelly down the sides of the jars to prevent any bubbles forming.

SAVOURY PRESERVES

All the basics of jam making apply when cooking savoury preserves as well. Generally, they are cooked until thick and pulpy, not watery, and when tested on a plate will leave a clean trail behind without any runny liquid. Choose firm, ripe and unblemished vegetables. Always use clean, warm jars and equipment, and refrigerate the preserve after opening.

Savoury preserves contain a variety of herbs and spices. It is key to remember that dried herbs and spices do lose their pungency if kept too long and this can affect the final flavour of the preserve. It is best to buy herbs and spices in small, not large, quantities.

Testing for flavour while the preserve is hot doesn't always give a true indication of the final flavour. The flavours will only develop after a few weeks' storage. For a quick idea of the taste, allow a little to cool on a saucer before trying it. Before making changes to a recipe, it is best to make it first as it is in the book. Any flavour adjustments can be made the next time you cook it.

CHUTNEYS

Long, slow cooking of both vegetables and fruit, with sugar, vinegar and spices so that the flavours and colours are both rich and concentrated, produce a thick, flavoursome pulp known as chutney. The flavour variations seem endless, depending on the fruit and vegetables used and the spices added.

Spices play a large part in chutney making and can change a plain chutney into a deliciously spicy aromatic one with the addition of chillies, cardamom and cinnamon, to name just a few. Just be careful not to add too many or you will overpower the flavours of the fruit in the chutney. Chutneys are cooked until very thick. They must be stirred often to prevent sticking and burning on the bottom of the pan. When tested on a plate, they should leave a clean trail behind without any runny liquid.

PICKLES

Preparing vegetables for pickling involves soaking them in a brine (salt and water solution) or layering them sprinkled with salt for 24 hours. The salt draws out moisture from the vegetables, which softens them and removes any excess liquid which may dilute the vinegar and adds flavour. Vegetables should be rinsed well under cold running water after salting. They can be left raw or lightly cooked and are packed into clean jars and topped with a vinegar solution. Spices can also be added to increase flavour.

RELISHES

The method for making relishes is very similar to that for making pickles. First salt the vegetables, then rinse them under cold, running water. The vegetable mixture is then simmered in a spicy vinegar solution before being thickened with cornflour or slurry—a thin paste made from plain flour and water.

CURDS

Gently cooked over a pan of simmering water, curds still require that the basics of jam making are followed. The combination of egg and butter thickens the fruit mixture both during cooking and once refrigerated.

FRUIT PASTES

Fruit pastes are a cross between jelly and jam. They are sieved fruit purées, cooked with sugar until thick and paste like. The basics of jam making apply, and great care is needed to avoid being splattered with the mixture as it bubbles in the base of the pan. Take care not to overcook it or let the mixture catch and burn on the bottom. Fruit pastes use a large amount of fruit, so it is best to make them when there is an overabundance.

DEFINITIONS

Jam Made from small pieces of fruit and sugar, cooked to a thick, spreadable consistency.

Preserve Whole fruits preserved in a heavy, sugar-based syrup.

Conserve Whole or large pieces of fruit cooked with sugar until thick in consistency.

Jelly Made from the strained juice of cooked fruits, and sugar. Generally clear, but can contain small pieces of the original fruit.

Marmalade Sliced, cooked citrus fruits, suspended in a sweet, thick jam mixture.

Fruit paste Sieved, cooked fruit, cooked to a thick paste with sugar and cut into pieces when cold.

Fruit curd Thick, spreadable, creamy mixture made with juice, fruit purée, and sometimes citrus rind, combined with sugar, eggs and butter and cooked until thick.

Pickle Vegetables, or sometimes fruit, pickled in vinegar with sugar, salt and spices.

Chutney Mixture of vegetables and/or fruit cooked with vinegar, sugar and spices to a thick, pulpy consistency.

Relish Salted cooked vegetables in a sugar, spice and vinegar-based sauce, which is thickened towards the end of cooking.

WHAT WENT WRONG?
Crystallization Too much sugar was added to the fruit, and it was not dissolved properly before boiling.

Tough fruit The fruit was not cooked long enough before the sugar was added. Fruit does not soften any further once the sugar is added.

Fruit floats The fruit was not cooked long enough or did not stand long enough before bottling.

Too runny Mixture has not set properly. Return it to pan, to the boil again and retest for setting point before bottling.

Mould Can start to grow once the jar is opened if storing in a warm place, or if the mixture was not covered while hot. If caught quickly, mould can be scooped off with a little jam and discarded. Refrigerate the remainder and eat as soon as possible.

Fermentation Mushy, overripe, bruised or damaged fruit were used in the cooking process, or not enough sugar was added to the fruit mixture. If you do use less sugar in a recipe, make sure you eat it within a few months because it won't keep as long. The set won't be quite as firm. Keep in the refrigerator after opening

Cloudiness This generally only occurs in jellies, when jelly bag was squeezed or disturbed while the fruit was dripping through.

STORAGE TIMES

Jams, conserves, preserves
Store in an airtight jar in a cool, dark place for 6–12 months. Once opened, refrigerate for up to 6 weeks.

Jellies
Store in an airtight jar in a cool, dark place for 6–12 months. Once opened, store in the refrigerator for 1 month.

Curds
Store in an airtight jar in the refrigerator for up to 2 weeks.

Fruit pastes
Set in disposable foil trays or wrap in greaseproof paper, then plastic wrap, then foil and then plastic wrap again.

Sauces, chutneys, relishes and pickles
They should be left for 1 month before eating to allow the flavours to fully develop. Store in a cool, dark place for up to 1 year. Once opened, store refrigerated for 6 weeks.

Heat-processed fruits and vegetables
Store in a cool, dark place for up to 1 year. Once opened, store in the refrigerator for 1 week.

Mustards
Store in a cool, dark place for up to 3 months. Once opened, refrigerate for 1–2 weeks.

sweet jams and preserves

Strawberry jam

1.5 kg (3 lb) strawberries
125 ml (4 fl oz/½ cup) lemon juice
1.25 kg (2 lb 12 oz/5½ cups) sugar, warmed

Put two small plates in the freezer (you may or may not need the second plate) for testing purposes. Wipe the strawberries clean and hull them. Place strawberries in a large pan with 125 ml (4 fl oz/½ cup) water, lemon juice and warmed sugar. Warm gently, without boiling, stirring carefully with a wooden spoon. Try not to break up the berries too much.

Increase the heat and, without boiling, continue to stir the mixture for 10 minutes, or until all the sugar has dissolved. Increase heat and boil for 20 minutes, stirring often. Skim any scum off surface with a skimmer or slotted spoon. Start testing for setting point after 20 minutes, but it may take up to 40 minutes. Be careful that the jam does not catch on the base of the pan and start to burn.

Remove from the heat, place a little jam onto one of the cold plates and place in the freezer for 30 seconds. When setting point is reached, a skin will form on the surface and the jam will wrinkle when pushed with your finger.

If ready, remove any scum from the surface. Spoon immediately into clean, warm jars and seal. Turn the jars upside down for 2 minutes, then invert and leave to cool. Label and date. Store in a cool, dark place for 6–12 months. Refrigerate after opening for up to 6 weeks.

If not ready, return jam to the heat for a few minutes and then test again, using the second plate.

NOTE: Do not wash strawberries once they have been hulled. They will absorb water and the taste will be affected.

Fig preserve

1 kg (2 lb 4 oz) fresh figs, stalks removed
125 ml (4 fl oz/½ cup) lemon juice
1 kg (2 lb 4 oz/4⅓ cups) sugar, warmed

Put two small plates in the freezer (you may or may not need the second plate) for testing purposes. Put the figs in a large heatproof bowl. Cover with boiling water for 3 minutes. Drain, cool and cut into pieces.

Place figs, lemon juice and 125 ml (4 fl oz/½ cup) water in a large pan. Bring to the boil, then reduce heat and simmer, covered, for 20 minutes, or until figs are soft.

Add the sugar and stir over medium heat, without boiling, for 5 minutes, or until all the sugar has dissolved.

Bring to the boil and boil for 20 minutes, stirring often. Remove any scum from the surface during cooking with a skimmer or slotted spoon. Add a little water if mixture thickens too much. When thick and pulpy, start testing for setting point.

Remove from the heat, place a little preserve onto one of the cold plates and place in the freezer for 30 seconds. When setting point is reached, a skin will form on the surface and the preserve will wrinkle when pushed with your finger.

If ready, remove any scum from the surface.Pour immediately into clean, warm jars, and seal. Turn the jars upside down for 2 minutes, then invert and leave to cool. Label and date. Store in a cool, dark place for 6–12 months. Refrigerate after opening for up to 6 weeks.

If not ready, return jam to the heat for a few minutes and then test again, using the second plate.

Mixed berry jam

1 kg (2 lb 4 oz) berries (strawberries, raspberries, blackberries,
blueberries, mulberries)
80 ml (2½ fl oz/⅓ cup) lemon juice
1 kg (2 lb 4 oz/4⅓ cups) sugar, warmed
25 g (1 oz) jam setting mixture

Place the berries and lemon juice in a large pan and gently cook for 10 minutes.
Add the sugar and stir over low heat for 5 minutes, or until all sugar has dissolved.

Boil for 15 minutes, stirring often, and remove from the heat. Add the jam setting
mixture, then return the berry mixture to the heat and boil rapidly for a further
5 minutes. Remove any scum from the surface with a skimmer or slotted spoon.

Pour immediately into clean, warm jars, and seal. Turn the jars upside down for
2 minutes, then invert and leave to cool. Label and date. Store in a cool, dark place
for 6–12 months. Refrigerate after opening for up to 6 weeks.

NOTE: Remove the stems, stalks, leaves and any blemishes from the berries you
have chosen. If the berries are sandy or gritty, wash them gently under cold water
and drain well in a colander before use. You can use a mixture of fresh and frozen
berries, if necessary.

Apricot and passionfruit jam

1.2 kg (2 lb 9 oz) fresh apricots, stones removed
1 kg (2 lb 4 oz/4⅓ cups) sugar, warmed
160 g (5¾ oz/⅔ cup) passionfruit pulp
2 tablespoons lemon juice

Put two small plates in the freezer (you may, or may not need the second plate) for testing purposes. Cut the apricots into quarters and then place in a large pan with 80 ml (2½ fl oz/⅓ cup) water. Cover and cook over low heat for 10 minutes, or until tender.

Remove from the heat and add the sugar, passionfruit pulp and lemon juice. Heat slowly, stirring, for 5 minutes, or until all sugar has dissolved. Return to the boil and boil rapidly for 30 minutes, stirring often. Remove any scum during cooking with a skimmer or slotted spoon. When the jam falls from a tilted wooden spoon in thick sheets without dripping, start testing for setting point.

Remove from the heat, place a little jam onto one of the cold plates and place in the freezer for 30 seconds. When setting point is reached, a skin will form on the surface and the jam will wrinkle when pushed with your finger.

If ready, remove any scum from the surface. Spoon immediately into clean, warm jars and seal. Turn the jars upside down for 2 minutes, then invert and leave to cool. Label and date. Store in a cool, dark place for 6–12 months. Refrigerate after opening for up to 6 weeks.

If not ready, return jam to the heat for a few minutes and then test again, using the second plate.

Raspberry jam

1.5 kg (3 lb 5 oz) fresh or frozen raspberries
80 ml (2½ fl oz/⅓ cup) lemon juice
1.5 kg (3 lb 5 oz/6½ cups) sugar, warmed

Place two plates in the freezer (you may or may not need the second plate) for testing purposes. Place the berries and lemon juice in a large pan. Stir over low heat for 10 minutes, or until the berries are soft.

Add sugar and stir, without boiling, for 5 minutes, or until all sugar has dissolved.

Bring the mixture to the boil and then boil, for 20 minutes. Stir often and make sure the jam doesn't stick or burn on the base of the pan. Remove any scum during cooking with a skimmer or slotted spoon. When the jam falls from a tilted wooden spoon in thick sheets without dripping, start testing for setting point.

Remove from heat, place a little jam onto one of the cold plates and place in the freezer for 30 seconds. When setting point is reached, a skin will form on the surface and jam will wrinkle when pushed with your finger.

If ready, remove any scum from the surface. Spoon immediately into clean, warm jars and seal. Turn the jars upside down for 2 minutes, then invert and leave to cool. Label and date. Store in a cool, dark place for 6–12 months. Refrigerate after opening for up to 6 weeks.

If not ready, return the jam to the heat for a few minutes and then test again, using the second plate.

NOTE: Frozen raspberries can be used, but the cooking time will increase.

Blueberry preserve

1 kg (2 lb 4 oz) blueberries
60 ml (2 fl oz/¼ cup) lemon juice (and the pips of 1 lemon)
1 kg (2 lb 4 oz/4⅓ cups) sugar, warmed

Put two small plates in the freezer (you may or may not need the second plate) for testing purposes. Place the blueberries in a large pan with 185 ml (6 fl oz/¾ cup) water. Place lemon pips on a piece of muslin (cheesecloth) and tie securely with string. Add to the pan. Cook over low heat for 5 minutes, or until the berries just start to colour the water.

Add the lemon juice and sugar, and stir over low heat for 5 minutes, or until all the sugar has dissolved. Bring slowly to the boil and cook for 20–25 minutes, stirring often. Remove any scum during cooking with a skimmer or slotted spoon. When the preserve falls from a tilted wooden spoon in thick sheets without dripping, start testing for setting point.

Remove from the heat, place a little preserve onto one of the cold plates and place in the freezer for 30 seconds. When setting point is reached, a skin will form on the surface and the preserve will wrinkle when pushed with your finger.

If ready, remove any scum from the surface. Transfer preserve to a heatproof jug and pour immediately into clean, warm jars and seal. Turn the jars upside down for 2 minutes, then invert and leave to cool. Label and date. Store in a cool, dark place for 6–12 months. Refrigerate after opening for up to 6 weeks.

If not ready, return jam to the heat for a few minutes and then test again, using the second plate.

Peach conserve

1.5 kg (3 lb 5 oz) peaches (about 9 large peaches)
1 green apple
1 lemon
1 kg (2 lb 4 oz/4⅓ cups) sugar, warmed

Put two small plates in the freezer. Score a cross in base of peaches. Place in a large heatproof bowl and cover with boiling water. Leave for 1–2 minutes, then remove, cool slightly and peel. Halve, remove stone and chop into 2 cm (1 inch) pieces.

Chop the apple, including peel and core, into 1 cm (½ inch) pieces. Peel thin strips of rind from the lemon, then cut it in half and juice. Place apple and lemon rind on a square of muslin (cheesecloth) and tie securely with string.

Place chopped peaches, 310 ml (11 fl oz/1¼ cups) water and muslin (cheesecloth) bag into a large pan. Bring slowly to the boil, then reduce the heat and simmer for 30 minutes, or until the peaches are tender. Remove any scum that forms on the surface. Squeeze any excess juice from the bag by pushing firmly against the side of pan, then discard it.

Add the sugar and stir over low heat for 5 minutes, or until sugar has dissolved. Add lemon juice, return to the boil and boil rapidly for 30 minutes, stirring often. Stir to check conserve is not sticking or burning. When conserve falls from a tilted wooden spoon in thick sheets without dripping, start testing for setting point.

Remove from heat, place a little conserve onto one of the cold plates and put in freezer for 30 seconds. When setting point is reached, a skin will form on surface and wrinkle when pushed with your finger.

If ready, remove any scum from the surface. Spoon immediately into clean, warm jars and seal. Turn upside down for 2 minutes, then invert and leave to cool. Label and date. Store in a cool, dark place for 6–12 months. Refrigerate after opening.

Tomato and pineapple jam

2 kg (4 lb 8 oz) ripe tomatoes
1.5 kg (3 lb 5 oz/6½ cups) sugar, warmed
125 ml (4 fl oz/½ cup) lemon juice
440 g (15¾ oz/2¾ cups) can crushed pineapple, drained

Put two small plates in the freezer (you may or may not need the second plate) for testing. Cut a cross in the base of the tomatoes, place in a large bowl, cover with boiling water and leave for 30 seconds, or until the skins start to spilt. Transfer the tomatoes to a bowl of cold water. Remove the skin and chop.

Place tomatoes in a pan. Add half the warmed sugar and simmer for 5–10 minutes over low heat, stirring, until the tomatoes have softened and sugar has dissolved.

Add the lemon juice, pineapple and remaining sugar. Stir over low heat until sugar has dissolved. Bring to the boil and cook for 30–35 minutes, stirring frequently. Remove any scum from the surface during cooking. When jam falls from a tilted wooden spoon in thick sheets without dripping, start testing for setting point.

Remove from heat, place a little jam onto one of the cold plates and put in freezer for 30 seconds. When setting point is reached, a skin will form on the surface and jam will wrinkle when pushed with your finger.

If ready, remove any scum from surface. Spoon immediately into clean, warm jars and seal. Turn jars upside down for 2 minutes, then invert and leave to cool. Label and date. Store in a cool, dark place for 6–12 months. Refrigerate after opening for up to 6 weeks.

NOTE: Ensure the tomatoes used are very ripe to maximise the taste of your jam. Vine-ripened tomatoes generally have the best flavour, however, they are also the most expensive.

Blood plum jam

2 kg (4 lb 8 oz) blood plums
125 ml (4 fl oz/½ cup) lemon juice
1.5 kg (3 lb 5 oz/6½ cups) sugar, warmed

Put two small plates in the freezer (you may or may not need the second plate) for testing purposes. Cut the plums in half and remove the stones. Place in a large pan and add 1 litre (4 cups) water. Bring slowly to the boil, then reduce the heat and simmer, covered, for 50 minutes, or until the fruit is soft.

Add lemon juice and sugar and stir over low heat, without boiling, for 5 minutes, or until all the sugar has dissolved. Bring to the boil and boil for 20 minutes, stirring often. Remove any scum from the surface during cooking with a skimmer or slotted spoon. When the jam falls from a tilted wooden spoon in thick sheets without dripping, start testing for setting point.

Remove from the heat, place a little jam onto one of the cold plates and place in the freezer for 30 seconds. When setting point is reached, a skin will form on the surface and the jam will wrinkle when pushed with your finger.

If ready, remove any scum from the surface. Spoon immediately into clean, warm jars and seal. Turn the jars upside down for 2 minutes, then invert and leave to cool. Label and date. Store in a cool, dark place for 6–12 months. Refrigerate after opening for up to 6 weeks.

If not ready, return the jam to the heat for a few minutes and then test again, using the second plate.

NOTE: Blood plums have dark skin and dark flesh. If they are not available, any kind of plum can be used.

Rhubarb and ginger jam

1.5 kg (3 lb 5 oz) trimmed rhubarb (leaves and ends removed)
1.5 kg (3 lb 5 oz) sugar, warmed
125 ml (4 fl oz/½ cup) lemon juice
4 cm (1½ inch) piece fresh ginger, bruised and halved
100 g (3½ oz) glacé ginger

Chop the rhubarb into small pieces. Layer the rhubarb, sugar and lemon juice in a large non-metallic bowl. Cover and leave overnight.

Put two small plates in the freezer (you may need more than one plate to test for setting point). Place the rhubarb mixture in a large pan. Finely chop the fresh ginger and place on a square of muslin (cheesecloth), tie securely with string and add to the pan. Stir over low heat for 5 minutes, or until all sugar has dissolved. Bring to the boil and boil rapidly for 20–30 minutes, stirring often. Remove any scum during cooking with a skimmer. When jam falls from a tilted wooden spoon in thick sheets without dripping, start testing for the setting point.

Remove from the heat, place a little jam onto one of the cold plates and put in the freezer for 30 seconds. When the setting point is reached, a skin will form on the surface and the jam will wrinkle when pushed with your finger.

If ready, remove any scum from the surface and discard muslin (cheesecloth) bag. Finely chop the glacé ginger and add to pan. Spoon immediately into clean, warm jars, and seal. Turn upside down for 2 minutes, then invert and leave to cool. Label and date. Store in a cool, dark place for 6–12 months. Refrigerate after opening for up to 6 weeks.

NOTE: The amount of ginger can be varied, according to taste.

Apricot jam

1 kg (2 lb 4 oz) apricots, stones removed, quartered
1 kg (2 lb 4 oz/4⅓ cups) sugar, warmed

Place two small plates in the freezer (you may or may not need the second plate) for testing purposes. Put apricots in a large pan and add 375 ml (13 fl oz/1½ cups) water. Bring to the boil, stirring, for 20 minutes, or until apricots have softened.

Add the sugar and stir, without boiling, for 5 minutes, or until all of the sugar has dissolved. Return to the boil and boil for 20 minutes, stirring often. Stir across the base of the pan to check that the jam is not sticking or burning. Remove any scum during cooking with a skimmer or slotted spoon. When the jam falls from a tilted wooden spoon in thick sheets without dripping, start testing for setting point.

Remove from heat, place a little jam onto one of the cold plates and put in freezer for 30 seconds. When setting point is reached, a skin will form on the surface and the jam will wrinkle when pushed with your finger.

If ready, remove any scum from the surface of the jam. Spoon immediately into clean, warm jars and seal. Turn the jars upside down for 2 minutes, then invert and leave to cool. Label and date. Store in a cool, dark place for 6–12 months. Refrigerate after opening for up to 6 weeks.

If not ready, return the jam to the heat for a few minutes and then test again, using the second plate.

Banana jam

1 kg (2 lb 4 oz) very ripe bananas (about 7), peeled (see note)
100 ml (3½ fl oz) lemon juice
750 g (1 lb 10 oz/3 cups) sugar, warmed

Put two small plates in the freezer (you may or may not need the second plate) for testing purposes. Chop the bananas and place in a large pan with the lemon juice and sugar. Bring to the boil and skim any scum from the surface with a skimmer or slotted spoon.

Cook the jam over medium heat for 30 minutes, then reduce the heat and simmer, stirring frequently, for 15–20 minutes, or until jam is thick and pale red in colour.

Remove from heat, place a little jam onto one of the cold plates and put in freezer for 30 seconds. When setting point is reached, a skin will form on the surface and the jam will wrinkle when pushed with your finger.

If ready, spoon immediately into clean, warm jars, and seal. Turn the jars upside down for 2 minutes, then invert and leave to cool. Label and date. Store in a cool, dark place for 6–12 months. Refrigerate after opening for up to 6 weeks.

If not ready, return the jam to the heat for a few minutes and then test again, using the second plate.

NOTE: Use old, mushy bananas, similar to those you would use for a banana cake. While not a true jam, it is just as delicious. Serve as you would other fruit jams.

Traditional fruit mince

2 large green apples (about
440 g/15½ oz), peeled, cored
and finely chopped
250 g (9 oz) packet suet mix
345 g (12 oz/1½ cups), firmly
packed soft brown sugar
375 g (13 oz/3 cups) raisins
250 g (9 oz/2 cups) sultanas
250 g (9 oz/2 cups) currants
150 g (5½ oz/¾ cup) mixed peel
100 g (3½ oz/¾ cup) slivered
almonds, chopped

1 tablespoon mixed spice
½ teaspoon nutmeg
½ teaspoon cinnamon
2 teaspoons grated orange rind
1 teaspoon grated lemon rind
250 ml (9 fl oz/1 cup) orange
juice
125 ml (8 fl oz/½ cup) lemon
juice
150 ml (5 fl oz) brandy

Combine all the ingredients and 125 ml (4 fl oz/½ cup) of the brandy in a large
bowl. Combine thoroughly.

Spoon the fruit mince into clean, warm jars. Use a skewer to remove air bubbles
and to pack the mixture in firmly. Leave a 1.5 cm (½ inch) space at the top of the
jar and wipe the jar clean with a cloth. Spoon a little brandy over the surface of the
fruit mince and seal. Label and date.

Set aside for at least 3 weeks, or up to 6 months, before using in pies and tarts.
You should keep the fruit mince refrigerated in hot weather.

Quick fruit mince

35 g (1¼ oz/¼ cup) currants
40 g (1½ oz/⅓ cup) sultanas
2 tablespoons mixed peel
30 g (1 oz/¼ cup) slivered
  almonds
1 apple, grated
45 g (1¾ oz/¼ cup) soft brown
  sugar
¼ teaspoon ground nutmeg
¼ teaspoon ground cinnamon

1 teaspoon grated orange rind
1 teaspoon grated lemon rind
100 g (3¾ oz/½ cup) can
  stoneless cherries, drained
  and quartered, or
  150 g (5½ oz/1 cup) fresh
  cherries, pitted
100 g (3½ oz/½ cup) white
  seedless grapes, halved
1 tablespoon whisky

To make the fruit mince mixture, combine all the ingredients in a large bowl and stir well.

Spoon into clean, warm jars and seal. Label and date.

NOTE: Use this quick fruit mince as a filling for mini tarts or as a topping for pancakes. It will only keep for a short period (up to 5 days in the refrigerator) because it is made with fresh fruit and has very little alcohol.

Frozen berry jam

300 g (10½ oz/2¼ cups) frozen blackberries
300 g (10½ oz/2¼ cups) frozen raspberries
300 g (10½ oz/2¼ cups) frozen blueberries
60 ml (2 fl oz/¼ cup) lemon juice, reserving any pips
750 g (1 lb 10 oz/3 cups) sugar, warmed

Put two small plates in the freezer (you may, or may nor need the second plate for testing). Put the frozen berries in a large pan with with 750 ml (26 fl oz/3 cups) water and the lemon juice.

Place the pips on a square of muslin (cheesecloth) and tie securely with string. Add to pan. Bring to the boil, then reduce the heat and simmer for 30 minutes.

Add the sugar and stir over low heat for 5 minutes, or until all sugar has dissolved. Return to the boil and boil for 30–40 minutes, stirring often. Remove any scum during cooking with a skimmer or slotted spoon. When the jam falls from a tilted wooden spoon in thick sheets without dripping, start testing for the setting point.

Remove from the heat, place a little jam onto one of the cold plates and place in the freezer for 30 seconds. A skin will form on the surface and the jam will wrinkle when pushed with your finger when setting point is reached. Discard the muslin (cheesecloth) bag.

If ready, remove any scum from the surface. Spoon immediately into clean, warm jars and seal. Turn the jars upside down for 2 minutes, then invert and leave to cool. Label and date. Store in a cool, dark place for 6–12 months. Refrigerate after opening for up to 6 weeks.

If not ready, return the jam to the heat for a few minutes and then test again, using the second plate.

Pineapple and mango jam

1 ripe pineapple
2 large mangoes
1 teaspoon lemon rind, grated
80 ml (2½ fl oz/⅓ cup) lemon juice, reserving the pips
   and skin of 1 lemon
1.2 kg (2 lb 9 oz/5 cups) warmed sugar

Place two small plates in the freezer (you may or may not need the second plate) for testing. Remove the skin and tough eyes from the pineapple. Cut into quarters lengthways, remove the core and cut the flesh into 1 cm (½ inch) pieces. Peel the mango and cut each mango cheek from the stone. Cut into 1 cm (½ inch) pieces. Place pineapple, mango, any juices, lemon rind and juice, and sugar in a large pan. Stir for 5 minutes, or until the sugar has dissolved.

Place the reserved pips and skin onto a square of muslin (cheesecloth) and tie securely with string. Add to the pan.

Bring to the boil, then reduce heat and simmer, stirring often, for 30–40 minutes, or until setting point is reached. Remove any scum that forms on the surface. Stir across base of the pan to check jam is not sticking or burning. When it falls from a tilted wooden spoon in thick sheets without dripping, start testing for setting point.

Remove from heat, place a little jam onto one of the cold plates and put in freezer for 30 seconds. A skin will form on the surface and jam will wrinkle when pushed with your finger when setting point is reached.

If ready, remove any scum from surface. Pour into clean, warm jars and seal. Turn upside down for 2 minutes, then invert and cool. Label and date. Store in a cool, dark place for 6–12 months. Refrigerate after opening for up to 6 weeks.

Blackberry and apple jam

750 g (1 lb 10 oz) green apples
1 kg (2 lb 4 oz/7½ cups) blackberries
1.5 kg (3 lb 5 oz/6½ cups) sugar, warmed

Put two small plates in the freezer (you may or may not need the second plate) for testing purposes. Peel, core and chop the apples. Place the apple pieces in a large pan with the berries and 125 ml (4 fl oz/½ cup) water. Cook, covered, over medium heat, stirring often, for 30 minutes, or until the fruit has softened.

Add sugar and stir, without boiling, for 5 minutes, or until the sugar has dissolved.

Bring the jam to the boil and boil for 20 minutes, stirring often. Stir across the base of pan to check it's not sticking or burning. When jam falls from a tilted wooden spoon in thick sheets without dripping, start testing for setting point

Remove from the heat, place a little jam onto one of the cold plates and place in the freezer for 30 seconds. A skin will form on the surface and the jam will wrinkle when pushed with your finger when setting point is reached.

If ready, remove any scum from the surface. Transfer to a heatproof jug and then immediately pour into clean, warm jars, and seal. Turn the jars upside down for 2 minutes, then invert and leave to cool. Label and date. Store in a cool, dark place for 6–12 months. Refrigerate after opening for up to 6 weeks.

If not ready, return the jam to the heat for a few minutes and then test again, using the second plate.

Melon and lemon conserve

2.5 kg (5 lb 8 oz) honeydew melons
6 lemons
1 tablespoon brandy
1.25 kg (2 lb 12 oz/5½ cups) sugar, warmed

Place two small plates in the freezer (you may or may not need the second plate) for testing purposes. Peel and seed the melons, then cut them into 1 cm (¼ inch) cubes and add to a large pan.

Scrub lemons under hot, running water with a soft bristle brush to remove wax coating, then cut them in half. Juice the lemons, retaining the pips, and add juice to the pan. Roughly chop lemons and divide the pieces and the pips between two squares of muslin (cheesecloth). Tie securely with string and add to the pan along with the brandy and 750 ml (12 fl oz/3 cups) water. Bring to the boil and boil for 40 minutes, or until the fruit is soft.

Add the sugar and stir over low heat, without boiling, for 5 minutes, or until all the sugar has dissolved. Bring to the boil and boil, stirring often, for 30 minutes. As the mixture thickens and starts to darken, reduce the heat and then simmer, stirring frequently, for 20–30 minutes. When conserve falls from a tilted wooden spoon in thick sheets without dripping, start testing for the setting point.

Remove from the heat, place a little conserve onto one of the cold plates and then put in freezer for 30 seconds. A skin will form on the surface and the conserve will wrinkle when pushed with your finger when setting point is reached. Discard the muslin (cheesecloth) bags.

If ready, remove any scum from the surface of the conserve .Spoon immediately into clean, warm jars and seal. Turn jars upside down for 2 minutes, then invert and leave to cool. Label and date. Store in a cool, dark place for 6–12 months. Refrigerate after opening for up to 6 weeks.

Black cherry jam

1 kg (2 lb 4 oz) fresh black cherries
125 ml (4 fl oz/½ cup) lemon juice
750 g (1 lb 10 oz/3 cups) sugar, warmed
25 g (1 oz) jam-setting mixture, if required

Put two small plates in the freezer (you may, or may not need the second plate) for testing purposes. Remove the stalks from cherries and, using a small sharp knife, cut cherries open and remove pips. Place the pips onto a square piece of muslin (cheesecloth) and tie securely with string.

Place cherries and muslin bag in a large pan together with 250 ml (9 fl oz/1 cup) water and the lemon juice. Bring to the boil, then reduce heat and simmer, stirring often, for 30 minutes, or until the cherries are tender. Discard the muslin bag.

Add the sugar and stir over low heat, without boiling, for 5 minutes, or until all the sugar has dissolved. Return to the boil and boil for 15–20 minutes, stirring often. Remove any scum with a skimmer or slotted spoon.

Remove from the heat, place a little jam onto one of the cold plates and place in the freezer for 30 seconds. A skin will form on the surface and the jam will wrinkle when pushed with your finger when setting point is reached. If the jam doesn't set, add the jam-setting mixture, return to the heat and boil rapidly for 5 minutes.

If ready, remove any scum from the surface. Spoon immediately into clean, warm jars and seal. Turn the jars upside down for 2 minutes, then invert and leave to cool. Label and date. Store in a cool, dark place for 6–12 months. Refrigerate after opening for up to 6 weeks.

NOTE: Cherries are low in pectin and jam-setting mixture is often added. If it is unavailable, boil the jam for a little longer and add more lemon juice.

Spiced dried peach conserve

400 g (14 oz) dried peaches, cut into 2 or 3 pieces
2 cinnamon sticks
3 cloves
3 cardamom pods
1.25 kg (2 lb 12 oz/5½ cups) sugar, warmed
60 ml (2 fl oz/¼ cup) lemon juice

Place dried peaches in a non-metallic bowl, add 1.75 litres (7 cups) water, cover and soak overnight.

Put two small plates in the freezer (you may or may not need the second plate) for testing purposes. Pour the peaches and the water into a large pan. Place spices on a square of muslin (cheesecloth) and tie securely with string. Add to the pan with 250 ml (9 fl oz/1 cup) water. Bring to the boil, reduce the heat and then simmer for 20 minutes, or until the fruit is soft.

Add sugar and lemon juice and stir over low heat, without boiling, for 5 minutes, or until dissolved. Return to the boil and boil for 20–25 minutes, stirring often. Remove any scum from surface during cooking. When conserve falls from a tilted wooden spoon in thick sheets without dripping, start testing for setting point.

Remove from the heat, place a little conserve onto one of the cold plates and place in the freezer for 30 seconds. A skin will form on the surface and the conserve will wrinkle when pushed with your finger when setting point is reached.

If ready, discard the bag. Remove any scum from the surface. Spoon immediately into clean, warm jars. Turn upside down for 2 minutes, then invert and leave them to cool. Label and date. Store in a cool, dark place for 6 –12 months. Refrigerate after opening for up to 6 weeks.

Boysenberry jam

1 kg (2 lb 4 oz/7½ cups) fresh boysenberries
80 ml (2½ fl oz/⅓ cup) lemon juice
1 kg (2 lb 4 oz/4⅓ cups) sugar, warmed

Put two small plates in the freezer (you may or may not need the second plate) for testing purposes. Place the berries and lemon juice in a large pan and cook gently for 10 minutes. Add sugar and stir over low heat for 5 minutes, or until all the sugar has dissolved.

Bring to the boil and then boil, stirring, for 20 minutes. Remove any scum with a skimmer or slotted spoon. When the jam falls from a tilted wooden spoon in thick sheets without dripping, start testing for setting point.

Remove from heat, place a little jam onto one of the cold plates and put it in the freezer for 30 seconds. A skin will form on the surface and the jam will wrinkle when pushed with your finger when setting point is reached.

If ready, remove any scum from the surface. Pour the jam immediately into clean, warm jars and seal. Turn jars upside down for 2 minutes, then invert and leave to cool. Label and date. Store in a cool, dark place for 6–12 months. Refrigerate after opening for up to 6 weeks.

If not ready, return the jam to the heat for a few minutes and then test again, using the second plate.

NOTE: If boysenberries are not available, any soft berry can be used, such as mulberries, raspberries, or blackberries.

Pear and ginger conserve

1.5 kg (3 lb 5 oz) beurre bosc pears
60 ml (2 fl oz/¼ cup) lemon juice
1 teaspoon grated lemon rind
1.5 kg (3 lb 5 oz) sugar, warmed
150 g (5 oz/⅔ cup) glacé ginger, finely chopped

Put two small plates in the freezer (you may or may not need the second plate) for testing purposes. Peel, halve and core the pears. Cut the flesh into 1.5 cm (½ inch) pieces. Place the cores and the seeds on a piece of muslin (cheesecloth), gather up and tie securely with string. Add to a large pan with the fruit, lemon juice and rind, and 250 ml (9 fl oz/1 cup) water.

Bring to the boil, then reduce the heat and simmer for 20–25 minutes, or until the pear is soft. Add the sugar and glacé ginger and stir over low heat, without boiling, for 5–10 minutes, or until the sugar has dissolved. Return to the boil and boil for 20–25 minutes, stirring often. Remove any scum during cooking with a skimmer or slotted spoon. When conserve falls from a tilted wooden spoon in thick sheets without dripping, start testing for setting point.

Remove from the heat, place a little conserve onto one of the cold plates and place in the freezer for 30 seconds. A skin will form on the surface and the conserve will wrinkle when pushed with your finger when setting point is reached. Discard the muslin (cheesecloth) bag.

If ready, remove any scum from the surface. Spoon the conserve immediately into clean, warm jars. Turn jars upside down for 2 minutes, then invert and leave them to cool. Label and date. Store in a cool, dark place for 6–12 months. Refrigerate after opening for up to 6 weeks.

If not ready, return the jam to the heat for a few minutes and then test again, using the second plate.

Winter fruit conserve

1.5 kg (3 lb 5 oz) firm pears, peeled and cored
1 grapefruit
1 orange
1 lemon
1.5 kg (3 lb 5 oz) sugar, warmed
250 g (9 oz/2 cups) raisins
60 g (2¼ oz/½ cup) sultanas
80 ml (2½ fl oz/⅓ cup) whisky

Put pears in a food processor. Scrub the grapefruit, orange and lemon under warm, running water with a soft bristle brush to remove the wax coating, then halve and thinly slice, removing the pips. Chop the flesh and add to the food processor with any juices. Process in batches until finely chopped and pulpy. Transfer the mixture to a large non-metallic bowl. Stir in the sugar, cover and leave overnight.

Place the mixture in a large pan and bring to the boil. Reduce the heat and simmer for 45 minutes, stirring often. Remove any scum during cooking with a skimmer or slotted spoon.

Add the raisins and sultanas and cook, stirring often, for 45 minutes, or until thick and pulpy. Remove from the heat and stir in the whisky.

Spoon immediately into clean, warm jars and seal. Turn the jars upside down for 2 minutes, then invert and leave to cool. Label and date. Store in a cool, dark place for 6–12 months. Refrigerate after opening for up to 6 weeks.

Black grape jam

1 kg (2 lb 4 oz/5½ cups) seedless black grapes (see note)
750 g (1 lb 10 oz/3⅓ cups) sugar, warmed
2 tablespoons lemon juice
50 g (1¾ oz) jam-setting mixture

Remove stems from grapes and place in a large pan with 80 ml (2 ½ fl oz/⅓ cup) water. Bring to the boil, then reduce the heat and simmer, covered, for 5 minutes.

Add the sugar and lemon juice and stir over low heat without boiling until all the sugar has dissolved.

Return to the boil and boil the jam rapidly for 10 minutes, stirring often. Remove any scum during cooking with a skimmer or slotted spoon. Add the jam-setting mixture and boil for a further 5 minutes. Remove any scum from the surface with a skimmer or slotted spoon.

Transfer to a heatproof jug and pour immediately into clean, warm jars, roughly dividing the whole grapes between the jars, and seal. Leave the jam to cool and, if possible, turn jars on their ends every 15–20 minutes in order to ensure that the grapes are evenly distributed throughout the jam. Label and date. Store in a cool, dark place for 6–12 months. Refrigerate after opening for up to 6 weeks.

NOTE: If using grapes with seeds, cut each grape in half and remove the seeds before continuing with the recipe.

Quince conserve

2 kg (4 lb 8 oz) quinces (about 5)
185 ml (6 fl oz /¾ cup) lemon juice
1.5 kg (3 lb 5 oz/4⅓ cups) sugar, warmed

Put two small plates in the freezer (you may or may not need the second plate) for testing purposes. Cut each quince into quarters then peel, core and cut into small cubes. Place fruit in a large pan with 2 litres (8 cups) water and lemon juice. Bring to the boil, reduce heat and simmer, covered, for 1 hour, or until fruit is soft.

Add the sugar and stir over low heat, without boiling, for 5 minutes, or until all the sugar has dissolved.

Return to the boil and boil, stirring often, for 25 minutes. Remove any scum during cooking with a skimmer or slotted spoon. When conserve falls from a tilted wooden spoon in thick sheets without dripping, start testing for setting point.

Remove from the heat, place a little conserve onto one of the cold plates and place in the freezer for 30 seconds. A skin will form on the surface and the conserve will wrinkle when pushed with your finger if setting point is reached.

If ready, remove any scum from the surface of the conserve with a skimmer or slotted spoon. Spoon immediately into clean, warm jars and seal. Turn upside down for 2 minutes, then invert and leave to cool. Label and date. Store in a cool, dark place for 6–12 months. Refrigerate after opening for up to 6 weeks.

If not ready, return the mixture to the heat for a few minutes and then test again, using the second plate.

NOTE: Quinces will turn from their natural yellow colour into a beautiful, rich red colour during cooking.

Dried apricot jam

500 g (1 lb 2 oz) dried apricots
1.5 kg (3 lb 5 oz/6½ cups) sugar, warmed
45 g (1¾ oz/⅓ cup) flaked almonds

Place the dried apricots in a large non-metallic bowl. Add 2 litres (8 cups) water and leave to soak overnight.

Put two small plates in the freezer (you may or may not need the second plate) for testing purposes. Pour the apricots and water into a large pan. Bring to the boil, then reduce the heat and simmer, covered, for 45 minutes, or until the fruit is soft.

Add the sugar and stir over low heat, without boiling, for 5 minutes, or until it has dissolved. Return to the boil and boil, stirring often, for 20–25 minutes. Remove any scum during cooking with a skimmer or slotted spoon. Stir frequently across the base of the pan to prevent jam from sticking. When the jam falls from a tilted wooden spoon in thick sheets without dripping, start testing for setting point.

Remove from the heat, place a little jam onto one of the cold plates and place in the freezer for 30 seconds. A skin will form on the surface and the jam will wrinkle when pushed with your finger when setting point is reached.

If ready, remove any scum from surface of the jam and add the flaked almonds. Spoon immediately into clean, warm jars and seal. Turn jars upside down for 2 minutes, then invert and leave to cool. Label and date. Store in a cool, dark place for 6–12 months. Refrigerate after opening for up to 6 weeks.

If not ready, return the mixture to the heat for a few minutes and then test again, using the second plate.

Tomato and passionfruit jam

2 kg (4 lb 8 oz) tomatoes
250 g (9 oz) passionfruit pulp (about 10 passionfruit)
60 ml (2 fl oz/¼ cup) lemon juice
2.5 kg (5 lb 8 oz/10¾ cups) sugar, warmed

Put two small plates in the freezer (you may or may not need the second plate) for testing purposes. Cut a cross at the base of the tomatoes, place in a large bowl, cover with boiling water and leave for 30 seconds, or until skins start to peel away. Transfer to a bowl of icy cold water, remove skins and roughly chop the tomatoes.

Put passionfruit pulp, lemon juice, tomato and any juices in a large pan. Bring to the boil, then reduce the heat and simmer for 15 minutes, or until thick and pulpy.

Add sugar and stir over low heat, without boiling, until all the sugar has dissolved. Return to the boil and boil for 30–40 minutes, stirring often. Remove any scum during cooking with a skimmer or slotted spoon. When the jam falls from a tilted wooden spoon in thick sheets without dripping, start testing for setting point.

If ready, remove from the heat, place a little jam onto one of the cold plates and place in the freezer for 30 seconds. A skin will form on the surface and jam will wrinkle when pushed with your finger when setting point is reached.

If ready, remove any scum from surface. Pour into clean, warm jars, and seal. Turn upside down for 2 minutes, then invert and leave to cool. Label and date. Store in a cool, dark place for 6–12 months. Refrigerate after opening for up to 6 weeks.

If not ready, return the mixture to the heat for a few minutes and then test again, using the second plate.

Fig and orange jam

185 ml (6 fl oz/¾ cup) orange juice
1.5 kg (3 lb 5 oz) fresh figs, chopped
60 ml (2 fl oz/¼ cup) lemon juice
2 tablespoons sweet sherry
1 kg (2 lb 4 oz/4⅓ cups) sugar, warmed

Put two small plates in the freezer (you may or may not need the second plate) for testing purposes. Place figs in a pan with orange juice, lemon juice and the sherry. Bring to the boil, reduce heat and simmer for 20 minutes, or until figs are soft.

Add sugar and stir over low heat, without boiling, until all the sugar has dissolved. Return to the boil and boil for 20–25 minutes, stirring often. Remove any scum during cooking with a skimmer or slotted spoon. When the jam falls from a tilted wooden spoon in thick sheets without dripping, start testing for setting point.

Remove from the heat, place a little jam onto one of the cold plates and put in the freezer for 30 seconds. A skin will form on the surface and jam will wrinkle when pushed with your finger when setting point is reached.

If ready, remove any scum from surface. Pour into clean, warm jars and seal. Turn upside down for 2 minutes, then invert and leave to cool. Label and date. Store in a cool, dark place for 6–12 months. Refrigerate after opening for up to 6 weeks.

If not ready, return mixture to the heat for a few minutes, then test again, using the second plate.

NOTE: Either dark or green-skinned figs can be used in this recipe.

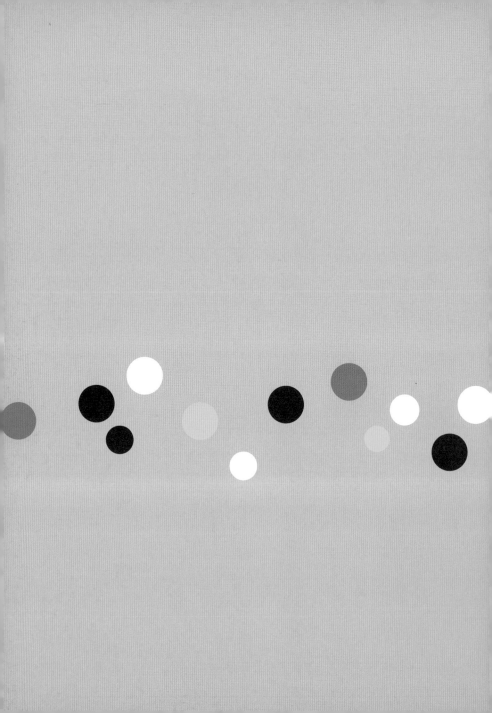

marmalades and jellies

Redcurrant jelly

600 g (1lb 4oz) redcurrants
600 g (1lb 4oz/2¾ cups) caster (superfine) sugar, warmed

Put two small plates in the freezer (you may, or may not need the second plate) for testing purposes. Place the redcurrants, including stems, and sugar in a pan. Crush the redcurrants to release the juices. Cook, stirring, over low heat, until all the sugar has dissolved.

Increase the heat and boil rapidly for 5 minutes, stirring often. Remove from heat, place a little jelly onto one of the cold plates and put in the freezer for 30 seconds. When setting point is reached, a skin will form on the surface and the jelly will wrinkle when pushed with your finger.

If ready, skim off any scum with a skimmer or slotted spoon and push the mixture through a fine sieve into a heatproof jug. Pour immediately into clean, warm jars and seal. Turn upside down for 2 minutes, then invert and leave to cool. Label and date. Store in a cool, dark place for 6–12 months. Refrigerate after opening for up to 6 weeks.

If not ready, return the mixture to the heat for a few minutes and then test again, using the second plate.

NOTE: For a shiny glaze and beautiful finish on sweet fruit tarts, melt a little jelly with water and brush over the top of the fruit. Or melt a spoonful in savoury sauces and gravies.

Dundee marmalade

1.5 kg (3 lb 5 oz) Seville oranges
2 lemons
1.5 kg (3 lb 5 oz/6½ cups) sugar,
   warmed

700 g (1 lb 9oz/3 cups) soft
   brown sugar
2 tablespoons treacle
2 tablespoons whisky, optional

Scrub the fruit under warm, running water with a soft bristle brush to remove the wax coating. Cut fruit in half, then cut again into quarters. Slice thinly, removing and retaining pips. Place pips on a square of muslin (cheesecloth) and tie securely with string. Place the fruit and the muslin bag in a large non-metal bowl. Pour in 1.75 litres (7 cups) water, cover with plastic wrap and leave overnight.

Put two small plates in the freezer (you may or may not need the second plate) for testing purposes.

Place the fruit and muslin bag in a large pan. Bring to the boil, then reduce the heat and simmer, covered, for 45 minutes, or until the fruit is tender.

Add sugars and treacle. Stir mixture over low heat, without boiling, for 5 minutes, or until sugar has dissolved. Return to the boil and boil rapidly for 30 minutes, stirring often. Remove any scum from surface. When marmalade falls from a tilted wooden spoon in thick sheets without dripping, start testing for setting point.

Remove from heat, place a little marmalade onto one of the cold plates and put in freezer for 30 seconds. When setting point is reached, a skin will form on surface and marmalade will wrinkle when pushed with your finger.

If ready, discard bag. Remove scum from surface. Stir in the whisky. Spoon into clean, warm jars and seal. Turn upside down for 2 minutes, then invert and leave to cool. Label and date. Store in a cool, dark place for 6–12 months. Refrigerate after opening for up to 6 weeks.

Quince jelly

2 kg (4 lb 8 oz) ripe yellow quinces
60 ml (2 fl oz/¼ cup) lemon juice
750 g (1 lb 10 oz/3½ cups) caster (superfine) sugar, warmed

Wipe the quinces clean, then cut into 5 cm (2 inch) pieces, including the skin and cores. Place quince pieces in a large pan with 2 litres (8 cups) water. Bring slowly to the boil, then reduce the heat and simmer, covered, for 1 hour, or until tender. Mash any firmer pieces with a potato masher.

Place a jelly bag in a bowl, cover with boiling water, drain and suspend the bag over a large heatproof bowl.

Ladle the fruit and liquid into the bag. Do not push the fruit through the bag or the jelly will become cloudy. Cover the top of the bag loosely with a clean tea towel, without touching the fruit mixture. Allow the mixture to drip through the bag overnight, or until there is no liquid dripping through the cloth.

Put two small plates in freezer (you may or may not need them both) for testing.

Discard the pulp from the fruit mixture and measure the liquid. Pour the liquid into a large pan and stir in lemon juice. Add 250 g (9 oz/1 cup) of warmed sugar for each 250 ml (9 fl oz/1 cup) of liquid. Stir over low heat for 5 minutes, or until the sugar has dissolved. Bring to the boil and boil rapidly for 20–25 minutes, stirring often. Skim any scum from the surface during cooking.

Start testing for setting point. Remove from heat, place a little jelly onto one of the cold plates and put in freezer for 30 seconds. When setting point is reached, a skin will form on the surface and the jelly will wrinkle when pushed with your finger.

If ready, remove any scum. Pour immediately down sides of clean, warm jars, and seal. Turn upside down for 2 minutes, invert and leave to cool. Store in a cool, dark place for 6–12 months. Refrigerate after opening for up to 6 weeks.

Three-fruit marmalade

1 grapefruit
2 oranges
2 lemons
3 kg (6 lb 12 oz/ 13 cups) sugar, warmed

Scrub fruit under warm, running water with a soft bristle brush to remove the wax coating. Quarter the grapefruit and halve the oranges and lemons, slice thinly and place in a non-metallic bowl. Retain pips and place them on a square of muslin (cheesecloth) and tie securely with string. Add the bag to the bowl with 2.5 litres (10 cups) water, cover and leave overnight.

Put two small plates in the freezer (you may or may not need the second plate) for testing purposes.

Put the fruit and water in a large pan. Bring to the boil, then reduce the heat and simmer, covered, for 1 hour, or until the fruit is tender.

Add sugar and stir over low heat, without boiling, for 5 minutes, or until all sugar has dissolved. Return to the boil and boil rapidly for 50–60 minutes, stirring often. Remove any scum during cooking. When marmalade falls from a tilted wooden spoon in thick sheets without dripping, start testing for setting point.

Remove from the heat, place a little marmalade onto one of the cold plates and place in the freezer for 30 seconds. When setting point is reached, a skin will form on the surface and the marmalade will wrinkle when pushed with your finger.

If ready, discard bag. Remove any scum from the surface. Spoon into clean, warm jars, and seal. Turn upside down for 2 minutes, then invert and leave to cool. Store in a cool, dark place for 6–12 months. Refrigerate after opening for up to 6 weeks.

If not ready, return the mixture to the heat for a few minutes and then test again, using the second plate.

Seville orange marmalade

4 Seville oranges (about 1.25 kg/2½ lb)
2–2.25 kg (4–4½ lb) sugar, warmed

Scrub oranges under warm, running water with a soft bristle brush to remove any wax coating. Cut the oranges in half, and then in half again. Slice oranges thinly, removing and retaining pips. Place pips on a square of muslin (cheesecloth) and tie securely with a piece of string. Place the orange and the bag in a large non-metallic bowl. Cover the fruit and pips with 2 litres (8 cups) water and leave overnight.

Put two small plates in freezer (you may or may not need them both) for testing.

Place the fruit and the bag in a large pan. Bring slowly to the boil, then reduce the heat and simmer, covered, for 45 minutes, or until the fruit is tender.

Measure the fruit and for every 250 ml (9 fl oz/1 cup) of fruit mixture add 250 g (9 oz/1 cup) of warmed sugar. Stir over low heat, without boiling, for 5 minutes, or until sugar has dissolved. Return to the boil and boil rapidly for 30–40 minutes, stirring often. Remove any scum from the surface during cooking with a skimmer or slotted spoon. When marmalade falls from a tilted wooden spoon in thick sheets without dripping, start testing for setting point.

Remove from heat, place a little marmalade onto one of the cold plates and put in the freezer for 30 seconds. When setting point is reached, a skin will form on the surface and the marmalade will wrinkle when pushed with your finger. Discard the muslin (cheesecloth) bag.

If ready, remove any scum from the surface. Spoon into clean, warm jars and seal. Turn upside down for 2 minutes, then invert and cool. Label and date. Store in a cool, dark place for 6–12 months. Refrigerate after opening for up to 6 weeks.

NOTE: Seville oranges are tropical or semi-tropical fruits that make great marmalade due to their thick, rough skin and tart flesh.

Grape jelly

2 kg (4 lb 8 oz) black seedless grapes
80 ml (2½ fl oz/⅓ cup) lemon juice, reserving any pips
550 g (1 lb 4 oz/2⅓ cups) sugar, warmed

Remove the stems from the grapes. Place the grapes in a large pan and add 250 ml (9 fl oz/1 cup) water. Place lemon pips onto a square of muslin (cheesecloth) and tie securely with string. Add to pan. Slowly bring to the boil, t hen reduce heat and simmer for 30–35 minutes, or until grapes are soft and pulpy. Remove and discard the muslin (cheesecloth) bag.

Place a jelly bag in a bowl, cover with boiling water, drain and suspend the bag over a large heatproof bowl.

Ladle the grape mixture into the jelly bag. Do not push the fruit through the bag or the jelly will become cloudy. Cover top of the bag loosely with a clean tea towel, without touching the fruit mixture, and allow the mixture to drip through the bag overnight, or until there is no liquid dripping through the cloth.

Discard the pulp and measure the liquid. Pour the liquid into a stainless steel or enamel pan and stir in the lemon juice. Add 185 g (6½ oz/¾ cup) sugar for each 250 ml (9 fl oz/1 cup) liquid. Stir over low heat until all sugar has dissolved, then bring to the boil and boil rapidly, stirring often, for 20–25 minutes, skimming any scum from the surface during cooking with a skimmer or slotted spoon.

Transfer to a heatproof jug and immediately pour the jelly down the sides of clean, warm jars and seal. Turn upside down for 2 minutes, then invert and leave to cool. Label and date. Store in a cool, dark place for 6–12 months. Refrigerate after opening for up to 6 weeks.

Cumquat marmalade

1 kg (2 lb 4 oz) cumquats
60 ml (2 fl oz/¼ cup) lemon juice
1.25 kg (2 lb 12 oz/5½ cups) sugar, warmed

Scrub cumquats under warm, running water with a soft bristle brush to remove wax coating. Remove and discard stems. Halve each lengthways, removing and retaining the pips, and slice finely. Place pips onto a square of muslin (cheesecloth) and tie securely with string. Put fruit and pips in a large non-metallic bowl. Add 1.25 litres (5 cups) water, cover with plastic wrap and leave overnight.

Put two small plates in the freezer (you may or may not need the second plate) for testing purposes. Place the cumquats and muslin (cheesecloth) bag in a large pan with the lemon juice. Bring slowly to the boil, then reduce the heat and simmer, covered, for 30 minutes, or until the fruit is tender.

Add the warmed sugar. Stir over low heat, without boiling, for 5 minutes, or until all the sugar has dissolved. Return the mixture to the boil and boil rapidly, stirring frequently, for 20 minutes. Skim any scum from the surface during cooking. When the marmalade falls from a tilted wooden spoon in thick sheets without dripping, start testing for setting point.

Remove pan from heat, place a little marmalade onto one of the cold plates and put in freezer for 30 seconds. A skin will form on the surface and the marmalade will wrinkle when pushed with your finger when setting point is reached.

If ready, discard bag. Remove any scum from surface. Spoon into clean, warm jars. Turn upside down for 2 minutes, invert and leave to cool. Label and date. Store in a cool, dark place for 6–12 months. Refrigerate after opening for up to 6 weeks.

If not ready, return mixture to heat briefly, then test again using the second plate.

Pomegranate jelly

2–2.5 kg (4–5 lb) pomegranates (about 8 pomegranates)
3 green apples
about 500 g (1 lb 2 oz/2⅓ cups) caster (superfine) sugar, warmed
60 ml (2 fl oz/¼ cup) lemon juice

Cut the pomegranates in half and use a juicer to squeeze the juice out of them. At least 500 ml (17 fl oz/2 cups) of pomegranate juice will be needed.

Chop apples, including skin and cores. Place in a large pan with the pomegranate juice and 250 ml (9 fl oz/1 cup) water. Bring slowly to the boil, then reduce the heat and simmer, covered, for 20 minutes, or until the apple is mushy.

Place a jelly bag in a large bowl, cover with boiling water, drain and suspend the bag over a large heatproof bowl. Ladle fruit and liquid into it. Do not push fruit through bag or jelly will become cloudy. Cover top of the bag with a tea towel, without touching fruit mixture. Allow mixture to drip through bag overnight.

Put two small plates in the freezer. Discard pulp from fruit mixture and measure liquid. Pour liquid into a large pan. Add sugar, 250 g (9 oz/1 cup) for every 250 ml (9 fl oz/1 cup) of liquid, and stir over medium heat until sugar has dissolved. Stir in lemon juice. Bring to the boil and boil rapidly for 15–20 minutes, stirring often. Skim any scum off the surface during cooking. Start testing for setting point.

Remove from the heat, place a little jelly onto one of the cold plates and put in the freezer for 30 seconds. A skin will form on the surface and the jelly will wrinkle when pushed with your finger when setting point is reached.

Remove scum from surface. Transfer jelly to a heatproof jug. Pour jelly down sides of jars to stop bubbles forming. Seal, turn upside down for 2 minutes, then invert and leave to cool. Store in a cool, dark place for 6–12 months. Refrigerate after opening for up to 6 weeks.

Cointreau orange marmalade

1 kg (2 lb 4 oz) oranges
2 kg (4 lb 8 oz/8½ cups) sugar, warmed
80 ml (2½ fl oz/⅓ cup) Cointreau

Scrub oranges with a soft bristle brush under warm, running water to remove the wax coating. Cut them in half, then into thin slices, reserving the pips. Place the pips on a square of muslin (cheesecloth) and tie securely with string. Place orange slices and muslin (cheesecloth) bag in a large non-metallic bowl along with 2 litres (8 cups) water, cover and leave overnight.

Put two small plates in the freezer (you may or may not need the second plate) for testing purposes. Transfer fruit, water and bag to a large pan. Bring slowly to the boil, then reduce the heat and simmer, covered, for 1 hour, or until fruit is tender and the mixture has reduced by a third.

Measure the fruit and for every 250 ml (9 fl oz/1 cup) of fruit mixture add 250 g (9 oz/1 cup) of warmed sugar. Stir over low heat, without boiling, for 5 minutes, or until sugar has dissolved. Bring to the boil and boil rapidly for 40–50 minutes, stirring often. Remove any scum from surface. When marmalade falls from a tilted wooden spoon in thick sheets without dripping, start testing for setting point.

Remove from the heat, place a little marmalade onto one of the cold plates and place in the freezer for 30 seconds. A skin will form on the surface and the marmalade will wrinkle when pushed with your finger when setting point is reached.

If ready, discard the muslin (cheesecloth) bag. Remove any scum from the surface. Stir in the Cointreau. Spoon immediately into clean, warm jars. Turn upside down for 2 minutes, then invert and leave to cool. Label and date. Store in a cool, dark place for 6–12 months. Refrigerate after opening for up to 6 weeks.

Lime marmalade

1 kg (2 lb 4 oz) limes
2.25 kg (5 lb/9¾ cups) sugar, warmed

Scrub the limes under warm, running water with a soft bristle brush to remove the wax coating. Cut in half lengthways, reserving any pips, slice thinly and place in a large non-metallic bowl with 2 litres (8 cups) water. Tie any lime pips securely in a square of muslin (cheesecloth) and add to the bowl. Cover and leave overnight.

Put two small plates in the freezer (you may or may not need the second plate) for testing purposes. Place the fruit and water in a large pan. Bring slowly to the boil, then reduce heat and simmer, covered, for 45 minutes, or until fruit is tender. Add the sugar and stir over low heat, without boiling, for 5 minutes, or until all sugar has dissolved. Return to the boil and boil rapidly, stirring often, for 20 minutes. Remove any scum that forms on surface during cooking with a skimmer or slotted spoon. When marmalade falls from a tilted wooden spoon in thick sheets without dripping, start testing for setting point.

Remove from the heat, place a little marmalade onto one of the cold plates and put in the freezer for 30 seconds. A skin will form on the surface and marmalade will wrinkle when pushed with your finger when setting point is reached.

If ready, discard the muslin bag. Remove scum from the surface using a skimmer or slotted spoon. Spoon immediately into clean, warm jars. Turn the jars upside down for 2 minutes, then invert and leave to cool. Label and date. Store in a cool, dark place for 6–12 months. Refrigerate after opening for up to 6 weeks.

If not ready, return the mixture to the heat for a few minutes and then test again, using the second plate.

NOTE: Look for brightly coloured limes that feel heavy for their size.

Grapefruit marmalade

1.25 kg (2 lb 12 oz) grapefruit (about 3 large)
2 lemons
2.5 kg (5 lb 8 oz/11 cups) sugar, warmed

Scrub the fruit under warm, running water with a soft bristle brush to remove the wax coating. Remove rind from fruit in long strips, avoiding the bitter white pith. Cut the strips into 5 cm (2 inch) lengths, then slice thinly. Remove the white pith from the fruit, then chop the flesh, discarding pips. Place all the fruit and rind in a large non-metallic bowl with 2.5 litres (10 cups) water; cover, leave overnight.

Put two small plates in the freezer (you may or may not need the second plate) for testing purposes. Place the fruit and water in a large pan, bring to the boil, then reduce the heat and simmer, covered, for 45 minutes, or until the fruit is tender.

Add the sugar and stir over low heat, without boiling, for 5 minutes, or until all sugar has dissolved. Return to the boil and boil, stirring often, for 40–50 minutes, checking frequently in the last 20 minutes. Remove any scum during cooking with a skimmer or slotted spoon. When marmalade falls from a tilted wooden spoon in thick sheets without dripping, start testing for setting point.

Remove from heat, place a little marmalade onto one of the cold plates and put in the freezer for 30 seconds. A skin will form on the surface and the marmalade will wrinkle when pushed with your finger when setting point is reached.

If ready, remove any scum from the surface. Spoon immediately into clean, warm jars and seal. Turn upside down for 2 minutes, then invert and leave to cool. Label and date. Store in a cool, dark place for 6–12 months. Refrigerate after opening for up to 6 weeks.

If not ready, return the mixture to the heat for a few minutes and then test again, using the second plate.

Apple and rose jelly

1.5 kg (3 lb 5 oz) apples
2 unsprayed roses
about 300 g (10½ oz/1⅓ cups) caster (superfine) sugar, warmed
2 teaspoons rose water

Chop the apples and put them in a pan with 1 litre (4 cups) water. Cook over low heat for 45 minutes, or until the apples have broken down into a purée.

Place a jelly bag in a bowl, cover with boiling water, drain and suspend the bag over a large heatproof bowl. Ladle the purée into the bag. Do not push the fruit through the bag or the jelly will become cloudy. Cover top of the bag loosely with a tea towel, without touching the fruit mixture. Allow mixture to drip through the bag overnight, or until there is no liquid dripping through the cloth.

Put two small plates in the freezer (you may or may not need the second plate) for testing. Pull the petals off the roses and wash gently in cold water. Discard pulp and measure the liquid. Pour liquid into a large pan and add 310 g (11 oz/1⅓ cups) warmed sugar for every 600 ml (21 fl oz/2⅓ cups) liquid. Stir over low heat until all sugar has dissolved. Bring to the boil and boil, stirring often, for 5–10 minutes. Skim off any scum on the surface. Start testing for setting point.

Remove from heat, place a little jelly onto one of the cold plates and place in the freezer for 30 seconds. A skin will form on the surface and the jelly will wrinkle when pushed with your finger when setting point is reached.

If ready, remove scum from surface. Stir in rose petals and rose water, then leave to cool until jelly begins to set (this will ensure rose petals are suspended in jelly).

Pour the jelly down the sides of clean, warm jars and seal. Turn upside down for 10 minutes, then slowly invert to disperse petals. Label and date. Store in a cool, dark place for 6–12 months. Refrigerate after opening for up to 6 weeks.

savoury jams and pickles

Onion and thyme marmalade

2 kg (4 lb 8 oz) onions, cut into rings
750 ml (26 fl oz/3 cups) malt vinegar
6 black peppercorns
2 bay leaves
805 g (1 lb 2 oz/3½ cups) firmly packed soft brown sugar
2 tablespoons fresh thyme leaves
10 x 3 cm (1¼ inch) sprigs fresh thyme

Place the onion in a large pan with the vinegar. Put the peppercorns and bay leaves on a square of muslin (cheesecloth) and tie securely with string. Add to the pan. Bring to the boil, then reduce the heat and simmer for 40–45 minutes, or until the onion is very soft.

Add the sugar, thyme leaves and 1 teaspoon salt. Stir until all sugar has dissolved. Bring to the boil, then reduce the heat and simmer, for 20–30 minutes, or until thick and syrupy. Skim any scum off the surface during cooking with a skimmer or slotted spoon.

Discard the muslin (cheesecloth) bag and stir in the fresh thyme sprigs. Spoon the onion pulp immediately into clean, warm jars, then pour in the syrup and seal the jars. Turn upside down for 2 minutes, then invert and leave to cool. Label and date. Leave for 1 month before opening to allow the flavours to develop. Store in a cool, dark place for up to 12 months. Refrigerate after opening for up to 6 weeks.

Chilli jam

500 g (1 lb 2 oz) red capsicums (peppers)
120 g (4¼ oz) red chillies
310 ml (10¾ fl oz/1¼ cups) white vinegar
1 kg (2 lb 4 oz/4¾ cups) sugar
185 g (6½ oz/¾ cup) lightly packed soft brown sugar

Remove the seeds and membrane from the capsicum and chilli. Cut the capsicum into large flattish pieces, and cook skin-side-up under a hot grill (broiler) until the skin blackens and blisters. Place in a plastic bag and cool, then remove the skin.

Put the capsicum and chilli in a food processor with 60 ml (2 fl oz/¼ cup) vinegar and process until finely chopped, in batches if necessary.

Put the capsicum and chilli mixture in a large pan and add the remaining vinegar. Bring to the boil, then reduce the heat and simmer for 8 minutes. Remove from the heat. Add the sugars and stir for 5 minutes, or until sugar has dissolved, then return to the heat and boil for 5–10 minutes, or until it has thickened slightly.

Spoon immediately into clean, warm jars and seal. Turn the jars upside down for 2 minutes, then invert and leave to cool. Label and date. Leave for 1 month before opening to allow the flavours to fully develop. Store in a cool, dark place for up to 12 months. Refrigerate after opening for up to 6 weeks.

Tomato sauce

2.5 kg (5 lb 8 oz) firm, ripe
   tomatoes
1 large onion
2 teaspoons black peppercorns
2 teaspoons whole cloves
2 teaspoons whole allspice
   (pimento)
1½ tablespoons tomato paste
   (purée)

4 cloves garlic, crushed
2 teaspoons ground ginger
¼ teaspoon cayenne pepper
600 ml (21 fl oz/2⅓ cups)
   white wine or cider vinegar
250 g (9oz/1 cup) sugar

Roughly chop the tomatoes and onion. Place the peppercorns, whole cloves and allspice on a square of muslin (cheesecloth) and tie securely with string.

Place tomato and onion in a large pan with the muslin (cheesecloth) bag, tomato paste, garlic, ginger, cayenne pepper, vinegar and 1 teaspoon salt. Bring slowly to the boil, then reduce the heat and simmer for 45 minutes.

Add sugar and stir over low heat for 5 minutes, or until all the sugar has dissolved.

Bring to the boil, then reduce the heat and simmer for 1 hour, or until the sauce is thick and pulpy. Stir frequently during cooking and watch that the mixture does not burn.

Discard the muslin (cheesecloth) bag. Place the mixture in a coarse sieve set over a large bowl, in batches if necessary. Use a metal spoon to press all the juices firmly from the pulp. Discard pulp and return the juice to the clean pan. Gently reheat the mixture for 10 minutes, then pour immediately into clean, warm jars or bottles and seal. Turn upside down for 2 minutes, then invert and leave to cool. Label and date. Leave for 1 month before opening to allow the flavours to develop. Store in a cool, dark place for up to 12 months. Refrigerate after opening for up to 6 weeks.

Preserved lemons

8–12 small thin-skinned lemons
310 g (11 oz/1 cup) rock salt
500 ml (17 fl oz/2 cups) lemon juice (8–10 lemons)
½ teaspoon black peppercorns
1 bay leaf
1 tablespoon olive oil

Scrub lemons under warm running water with a soft bristle brush to remove the wax coating. Cut into quarters, leaving the base attached at the stem end. Gently open each lemon, remove any visible pips and pack 1 tablespoon of salt against the cut edges of each lemon. Push lemons back into shape and pack tightly into a 2 litre (8 cup) jar with a clip or tight-fitting lid. (Depending on the size of lemons, you may not need all 12. They should be firmly packed and fill the jar.

Add 250 ml (9 fl oz/1 cup) of the lemon juice, remaining rock salt, peppercorns and bay leaf to the jar. Fill the jar to the top with the remaining lemon juice. Seal and shake to combine all the ingredients. Leave in a cool, dark place for 6 weeks, inverting each week. (In warm weather, store in the refrigerator.) The liquid will be cloudy initially, but will clear by the fourth week.

To test if the lemons are preserved, cut through the centre of one of the lemon quarters. If the pith is still white, the lemons are not ready. Re-seal and leave for another week before testing again.

Once the lemons are preserved, cover the brine with a layer of olive oil. Replace the oil each time you remove some of the lemon.

NOTE: Serve the lemons with grilled meats or use to flavour couscous, stuffings, tagines and casseroles. Only the rind is used in cooking. Discard the flesh, rinse and finely slice or chop the rind before adding to the dish.

Indian lime pickle

10 firm yellow/pale green limes
185 ml (6 fl oz/¾ cup) oil
1 teaspoon fenugreek seeds
¾ teaspoon ground turmeric
3 teaspoons chilli powder
1 teaspoon asafoetida powder

Wash the limes and dry thoroughly. Heat 60 ml (2 fl oz/¼ cup) oil in a pan. Add 2 limes and cook over low heat, turning often, for 2 minutes. Remove and repeat until all the limes are done. Do not allow the skin to turn brown. Cool, then cut each lime into eight wedges and cut each wedge into three. Discard the seeds and reserve any juice.

In a dry pan, heat the fenugreek seeds for 1 minute, or until the colour lightens. Take care not to burn the seeds as this will make the pickle bitter. Grind to a fine powder in a mortar and pestle or spice mill.

Heat the remaining oil in a heavy-based pan. Add the turmeric, the chilli powder, asafoetida and 1 tablespoon salt. Stir quickly and add the limes and reserved juice. Turn off the heat, add the ground fenugreek and stir well.

Spoon immediately into clean, warm jars. Pour a thin layer of warmed oil into each bottle. Seal, label and date. Leave for 1 month before opening to allow the flavours to develop. Store in a cool, dark place for up to 12 months. Refrigerate after opening for up to 6 weeks.

NOTE: Dark green limes are too acidic so use pale green/yellow ones. The rind softens with time. Asafoetida powder is a dried plant resin with a strong garlicky smell and is available from Indian spice stores.

Thai sweet chilli sauce

150 g (5½ oz) medium–large fresh red chillies
210 g (7½ oz/1⅔ cups) sultanas
3 cloves garlic, chopped
3 cm (1½ inches) finely grated fresh ginger
250 ml (9 fl oz/1 cup) white vinegar
410 g (14½ oz/1¾ cups) sugar
150 g (5½ oz/ ⅔ cup) firmly packed soft brown sugar
1 tablespoon fish sauce

Wearing latex or rubber gloves to protect your hands, cut the chillies in half and remove the seeds.

Combine the chilli, sultanas, garlic, ginger and 60 ml (2 fl oz/¼ cup) of the vinegar in a food processor or blender and process until smooth.

Place chilli mixture in a large pan, stir in the remaining vinegar, white and brown sugar, fish sauce, ¼ teaspoon salt and 100 ml (3½ fl oz) water. Bring to the boil, stirring until all the sugar has dissolved, then reduce the heat and simmer, stirring often, for 15 minutes, or until the mixture is a slightly thick, syrupy consistency.

Pour immediately into clean, warm jars or bottles and seal. Turn the jars upside down for 2 minutes, then invert and cool. Label and date. Leave for 1 month before opening to allow the flavours to develop. Store in a cool, dark place for up to 12 months. Refrigerate after opening for up to 6 weeks.

NOTE: This sauce is quite sweet, yet has a good bite. If you prefer a milder sauce, you can adjust the amount of chilli to your taste. The seeds contain the most heat, so remember to remove these. Wearing gloves helps prevent any irritation to sensitive skin which can sometimes occur when dealing with chillies.

Green tomato pickles

1.25 kg (2 lb 12 oz) green tomatoes
2 onions
120 g (4¼ oz) cooking salt
250 g (9 oz/1¼ cups) sugar
500 ml (17 fl oz/2 cups) cider vinegar
60 g (2¼ oz/½ cup) sultanas
½ teaspoon mixed spice
½ teaspoon ground cinnamon
2 teaspoons curry powder
pinch cayenne pepper
2 teaspoons cornflour (cornstarch)

Slice the tomatoes and onions into thin rounds. Combine with the salt in a large non-metallic bowl and add enough water to cover. Place a small plate on top of the vegetables to keep them submerged. Leave to stand overnight.

Drain the tomato and onion and rinse well. Place in a large pan and add the sugar, the vinegar, the sultanas and the spices. Stir over low heat for 5 minutes, or until all the sugar has dissolved.

Bring to the boil, then reduce the heat and simmer for 30 minutes, stirring often, or until the vegetables are soft.

Add 2 teaspoons water to the corn-flour, mix well and and stir into the mixture. Stir over medium heat until it boils and thickens.

Spoon immediately into clean, warm jars and seal. Turn the jars upside down for 2 minutes, then invert and leave to cool. Label and date. Leave for 1 month before opening to allow the flavours to develop fully. Store in a cool, dark place for up to 12 months. Refrigerate after opening for up to 6 weeks.

Okra pickles

420 ml (14½ fl oz/1⅔ cups) cider vinegar
1 teaspoon coriander (cilantro) seeds
1 teaspoon mustard seeds
1 cinnamon stick
4–6 dried small red chillies
2 tablespoons soft brown sugar
1 onion, chopped
500 g (1 lb 2 oz) small okra, chopped into 1 cm (½ inch) pieces

Place the vinegar, spices, chillies, sugar and 1½ tablespoons water in a large pan and bring to the boil. Reduce heat and simmer for 5 minutes, then remove from the heat, cover and infuse for 25 minutes.

Strain vinegar mixture, reserving the chillies, then return to the pan. You will need about 375 ml (13 fl oz/1½ cups) of liquid. Add the onion and okra, 2 tablespoons salt and bring to the boil. Reduce heat and simmer over low heat for 5 minutes, or until the okra is half cooked and there is no more of the sliminess that it releases. Skim off any scum on the surface during cooking.

Strain the okra and onion mixture, reserving the liquid, and then pack the mixture immediately into clean, warm jars, adding two of the reserved chillies to each jar. Fil jars with the reserved pickling liquid and seal. Turn upside down for 2 minutes, then invert and leave to cool. Label and date. Leave for 1 month before opening to allow the flavours to fully develop. Store in a cool, dark place for up to 12 months. Refrigerate after opening for up to 6 weeks.

NOTE: Use small okra as the larger, older ones tend to be more fibrous. The okra will start to absorb the liquid after 1–2 weeks.

Plum sauce

1 large green apple
2 red chillies
1.25 kg (2 lb 12 oz) blood plums, halved
450 g (1 lb/2 cups) firmly packed soft brown sugar
375 ml (13 fl oz/1½ cups) white wine vinegar
1 onion, grated
60 ml (2 fl oz/¼ cup) soy sauce
2 tablespoons fresh ginger, finely chopped
2 cloves garlic, crushed

Peel, core and chop the apple and place in a large pan with 125 ml (4 fl oz/½ cup) water. Cover and simmer for 10 minutes, or until the apple is soft. Cut the chillies in half lengthways. Remove seeds and chop finely. Add the plums, sugar, vinegar, onion, soy sauce, ginger, garlic and the chilli.

Bring the mixture to the boil and cook, uncovered, over low–medium heat for 45 minutes. Stir the mixture often throughout the cooking process. Remove the sauce from the pan and press it through a coarse strainer set over a large bowl using a wooden spoon. Discard the plum stones. Rinse the pan. Put the sauce back in the clean pan and return to the heat.

Cook sauce rapidly while stirring until it has thickened slightly—the sauce will thicken even further on cooling.

Pour immediately into clean, warm jars and seal. Turn the jars upside down for 2 minutes, then invert and leave to cool. Label and date. Leave for 1 month prior to opening to allow the flavours to develop. Store in a cool, dark place for up to 12 months. Refrigerate after opening for up to 6 weeks.

Chilli and garlic sauce

8 large dried chillies
4 medium fresh red chillies
4 cloves garlic
125 ml (4 fl oz/½ cup) white vinegar
185 g (6½ fl oz/¾ cup) sugar
1 tablespoon fish sauce

Remove the stem and seeds from the dried chillies, and break into large pieces. Place in a bowl, cover with boiling water and soak for 15 minutes.

Meanwhile, cut the fresh chillies in half and remove the seeds. Wear gloves to protect your hands. Finely chop garlic. Drain the dried chilli and place in a food processor or blender with the fresh chilli and vinegar. Process until smooth.

Pour into a pan and bring to the boil, then reduce the heat, stir in sugar and garlic, and simmer for 10 minutes, stirring often, until slightly thickened. Add fish sauce.

Transfer to a heatproof jug and pour immediately into clean, warm jars and seal. Turn jars upside down for 2 minutes, then invert and cool. Label and date. Leave for 1 month before opening to allow the flavours to develop. Store in a cool, dark place for up to 12 months. Refrigerate after opening.

NOTE: The heat in the chilli depends on the chillies used and their size. Usually, the smaller the chilli the hotter it is.

Red capsicum sauce

2 kg (4 lb 8 oz) red capsicums (peppers)
2 tomatoes
1 large onion, chopped
1 small green apple, peeled, cored and chopped
165 g (5¾ oz/¾ cup) firmly packed soft brown sugar
500 ml (17 fl oz/2 cups) cider vinegar
2 teaspoons black peppercorns
2 tablespoons roughly chopped fresh basil leaves
1 teaspoon cloves
1 bay leaf
3 cloves garlic

Preheat oven to 200°C (400°F/ Gas 6). Roast capsicums for 35 minutes, or until skin blisters and blackens. Cut into quarters, remove skins, seeds and membrane, and chop flesh. Score a cross in the base of the tomatoes, put in a heatproof bowl and cover with boiling water for 30 seconds. Transfer to cold water and peel the skin away from the cross. Roughly chop the flesh.

Put capsicum, tomato, onion and apple in a food processor or blender and process until finely chopped. Place in a large pan along with sugar, vinegar and 1 teaspoon salt. Put the peppercorns, basil, cloves, bay leaf and garlic onto a square piece of muslin (cheesecloth), tie with string and add to the pan.

Stir over low heat until sugar has dissolved. Bring to the boil, then reduce the heat and simmer, stirring often, over low–medium heat, for 1 hour 15 minutes, or until the sauce is thick and pulpy. Process in a food processor or blender until smooth.

Pour immediately into clean, warm bottles or jars and seal. Turn upside down for 2 minutes, then invert and leave to cool. Leave for 1 month before opening. Store in a cool, dark place for up to 12 months. Refrigerate after opening.

Eggplant pickle

800g (1 lb 12 oz) eggplant (aubergine), cut into 1 cm (½ inch) cubes
4 cloves garlic, chopped
50 g (1¾ oz) fresh ginger, chopped
2 red chillies, chopped
125 ml (4 fl oz/½ cup) oil
1 onion, chopped
1 tablespoon ground cumin
1 teaspoon fennel seeds
1 tablespoon ground coriander
½ teaspoon ground turmeric
250 ml (9 fl oz/1 cup) white wine vinegar
165 g (5¾ oz/¾ cup) sugar

Put the eggplant in a colander set over a bowl and sprinkle with 1 tablespoon salt. Leave for 20 minutes, then rinse well in cold water and pat dry with paper towels.

Chop the garlic, ginger and chilli in a food processor, adding a teaspoon of water if necessary, to make a paste.

Heat the oil in a large pan, add onion and cook for 2 minutes, or until soft. Add the garlic paste and ground cumin, fennel seeds, ground coriander and turmeric, and cook, stirring, for 1 minute. Add the eggplant and cook for 5–10 minutes, or until the eggplant has softened.

Add the white wine vinegar, sugar and 1 teaspoon salt, if necessary, and stir to combine. Cover and simmer gently for 15 minutes, or until soft.

Spoon immediately into clean, warm jars. Use a skewer to remove any air bubbles and seal. Turn the jars upside down for 2 minutes, then invert and leave to cool. Label and date. Leave for 1 month to allow the flavours to develop. Store in a cool, dark place for up to 12 months. Refrigerate after opening for up to 6 weeks.

chutneys and relishes

Spicy dried fruit chutney

400 g (14 oz) dried apricots
200 g (7 oz) dried peaches
200 g (7 oz) dried pears
250 g (9 oz) raisins
200 g (7 oz) pitted dates
250 g (9 oz) onions
250 g (9 oz) green apples, peeled and cored
4 cloves garlic, finely chopped
1 teaspoon ground cumin
1 teaspoon ground coriander
1 teaspoon ground cloves
1 teaspoon ground cayenne pepper
600 g (1 lb 5 oz/2⅔ cups) lightly packed soft brown sugar
600 ml (21 fl oz) malt vinegar

Finely chop apricots, peaches, pears, raisins, dates, onions and apples. Put in a large pan. Add garlic, cumin, coriander, cloves, cayenne pepper, sugar, vinegar, 2 teaspoons salt and 750 ml (26 fl oz/3 cups) water to the pan.

Stir over low heat until all the sugar has dissolved. Increase the heat and bring to the boil, then reduce the heat and simmer, stirring often, over medium heat for 1½ hours, or until mixture has thickened and fruit is soft and pulpy. Do not cook over high heat because the liquid will evaporate too quickly and the flavours will not have time to fully develop.

Spoon immediately into clean, warm jars, and seal. Turn the jars upside down for 2 minutes, then invert and leave to cool. Label and date. Leave for 1 month before opening to allow the flavours to fully develop. Store in a cool, dark place for up to 12 months. Refrigerate after opening.

Green mango chutney

2.6 kg (5 lb 12 oz) firm green mangoes (about 6 medium size)
1 large onion, finely chopped
170 ml (5½ fl oz/⅔ cup) white vinegar
115 g (4 oz/½ cup) firmly packed soft brown sugar
185 g (6½ fl oz/¾ cup) sugar
2 teaspoons ground ginger
2 teaspoons garam marsala

Remove the peel from the mangoes. Cut the cheeks from the rounded side of each mango and the small amount of flesh around the sides of the seed. Chop the flesh into 1 cm (½ inch) pieces and place in a large pan.

Add the remaining ingredients and 1 teaspoon salt to the pan. Stir over medium heat, without boiling, for 5 minutes, or until all the sugar has dissolved.

Bring to the boil, then reduce the heat and simmer for about 45 minutes, or until mixture is very thick and pulpy. Stir often during cooking to prevent the chutney from sticking and burning on the bottom of the pan, especially towards the end of the cooking time.

Spoon immediately into clean, warm jars and seal. Turn the jars upside down for 2 minutes, then invert and leave to cool. Label and date. Leave for 1 month before opening to allow the flavours to develop. Store in a cool, dark place for up to 12 months. Refrigerate after opening for up to 6 weeks.

NOTE: This chutney is a traditional accompaniment to Indian-style dishes. Choose firm, green mangoes without bruises or blemishes.

Chow chow

650 g (1 lb 7 oz/5 ⅓ cups) cauliflower, cut into small florets

1 Lebanese (short) cucumber, peeled, seeded and cut into 2 cm (¾ inch) cubes

375 g (13 oz/3 cups) green beans, trimmed and cut into 3 cm (1¼ inch) lengths

1 red and 1 green capsicum (pepper), cut into cubes

1 litre (4 cups) cider vinegar

230 g (8 oz/1 cup) firmly packed soft brown sugar

2 tablespoons mustard powder

2 tablespoons yellow mustard seeds

2 teaspoons ground turmeric

pinch cayenne pepper

60 g (2¼ oz) plain (all-purpose) flour

420 g (15 oz) can red kidney beans, rinsed and drained

310 g (11 oz/1½ cups) can corn kernels, drained

Blanch the cauliflower florets, cucumber, beans and capsicum separately in boiling water. Drain and cool quickly under cold running water. Set aside.

Reserve 250 ml (9 fl oz/1 cup) of the vinegar. Combine the remaining vinegar with the sugar, mustard powder and seeds, turmeric and cayenne pepper in a large pan. Stir over low heat to dissolve the sugar.

Whisk the reserved vinegar and the flour together in a bowl. Add to the pan and whisk over medium heat for 5 minutes, or until the mixture boils and thickens. Add the blanched vegetables, kidney beans and corn kernels. Mix thoroughly, bring to the boil, and cook, stirring often, for another 5 minutes.

Spoon immediately into clean, warm jars and seal. Turn the jars upside down for 2 minutes, then invert and leave to cool. Label and date. Leave for 1 month before opening to allow the flavours to develop. Store in a cool, dark place for up to 12 months. Refrigerate after opening for up to 6 weeks.

Nectarine and lemon grass chutney

3 large green chillies
3 stalks lemon grass, white part only
1.5 kg (3 lb 5 oz) nectarines, stones removed, roughly chopped
3 cloves garlic, finely chopped
2 tablespoons grated fresh ginger
1 large onion, chopped
2 teaspoons ground coriander
500 ml (17 fl oz/2 cups) white wine vinegar
280 g (10 oz/1⅓ cups) lightly packed soft brown sugar

Cut the chillies in half, remove the seeds from two and finely slice all the chillies. Bruise the lemon grass with the back of a knife and slice finely.

Place all the ingredients in a large pan and add 1 teaspoon salt. Stir over low heat for 5 minutes, or until all the sugar has dissolved.

Bring to the boil, then reduce the heat and simmer for 45–50 minutes, or until the chutney is thick and pulpy. Stir often to prevent chutney from sticking or burning on the bottom.

Spoon immediately into clean, warm jars and seal. Turn the jars upside down for 2 minutes, then invert and leave to cool. Label and date. Leave for 1 month before opening to allow the flavours to fully develop. Store in a cool, dark place for up to 12 months. Refrigerate after opening for up to 6 weeks.

NOTE: Wear gloves when handling the chillies to protect your fingers.

Chilli and red capsicum relish

4 large red capsicums (peppers)
2 large onions, roughly chopped
1 red chilli
2 cloves garlic
500 ml (17 fl oz/2 cups) white vinegar
1.5 kg (3 lb 5 oz/6½ cups) sugar, approximately

Quarter the capsicums and remove the seeds and white membrane. Roughly chop and place in a food processor or blender with the onion, chilli, garlic and some salt. You may need to do this in batches. Process until smooth and place in a large pan.

Add vinegar, bring to the boil and boil for 10–15 minutes, or until tender. Measure the capsicum mixture and measure an equal amount of sugar. Add the sugar to the mixture, stirring until it has dissolved, and slowly bring to the boil. Brush down the sides of the pan with a wet brush to remove any undissolved sugar. Remove any scum during cooking with a skimmer or slotted spoon.

Boil for 15 minutes, stirring often, then reduce heat and simmer for 30 minutes, or until the relish is thick and pulpy.

Spoon immediately into clean, warm jars and seal. Turn the jars upside down for 2 minutes, then invert and cool. Label and date. Leave for 1 month before opening to allow the flavours to develop. Store in a cool, dark place for up to 12 months. Refrigerate after opening for up to 6 weeks.

NOTE: Brushing the sides of the pan dissolves any sugar crystals which, if left, could cause the relish to crystallize when chilled.

Banana, tamarind and date chutney

125 g (4½ oz) tamarind pulp
90 g (3¼ oz/⅓ cup) caster (superfine) sugar
1 teaspoon ground cumin
½ teaspoon cayenne pepper
2 tablespoons grated fresh ginger
250 g (9 oz/1½ cups) pitted dates, chopped
60 g (2¼ oz/½ cup) slivered almonds
8 firm ripe bananas, chopped

Put the tamarind pulp in a bowl with 750 ml (26 fl oz/3 cups) boiling water. Cool, then break up with a fork. Pour into a sieve placed over a bowl and press out the liquid. Discard the seeds.

Put the liquid in a large pan with the sugar, cumin, cayenne pepper and 1 teaspoon salt. Stir over low heat until all the sugar has dissolved.

Add the ginger, dates and almonds. Bring to the boil, then reduce the heat and simmer for 10 minutes. Add the banana and cook, stirring often, for 30 minutes, or until soft and pulpy.

Spoon immediately into clean, warm jars. Use a metal skewer to remove any air bubbles and seal. Turn upside down for 2 minutes, then invert and leave to cool. Label and date. Leave for 1 month before opening to allow flavours to develop. Store in a cool, dark place for up to 12 months. Refrigerate after opening for up to 6 weeks.

NOTE: Tamarind pulp is available in most Asian grocery stores.

Banana
Tamarind
& Date
Chutney

Blueberry relish

1 kg (2 lb 4 oz/6½ cups) blueberries
500 g (1 lb 2 oz/2 cups) sugar
185 ml (6 fl oz/¾ cup) white wine vinegar
1 teaspoon cayenne pepper
½ teaspoon ground allspice (pimento)
¼ teaspoon ground cinnamon
60 ml (2 fl oz/¼ cup) lemon juice (reserve any pips and rind)

Place the blueberries in a large pan along with the sugar, vinegar, cayenne pepper, allspice, cinnamon, lemon juice, 1 teaspoon salt and 125 ml (4 fl oz/½ cup) water. Roughly chop the rind of half a lemon and, with the pips, place onto a square of muslin (cheesecloth) and tie securely with string. Add to the pan.

Stir over low heat for 5 minutes, or until all the sugar has dissolved.

Bring to the boil, reduce the heat and simmer, stirring often, for 50–55 minutes, or until the relish is thick and syrupy.

Spoon immediately into clean, warm jars and seal. Turn the jars upside down for 2 minutes, then invert and leave to cool. Label and date. Leave for 1 month before opening to allow the flavours to fully develop. Store in a cool, dark place for up to 12 months. Refrigerate after opening for up to 6 weeks

NOTE: Blueberries are delicate fruit, so be careful not to overcook them or they will break up and fall apart.

Roast peach chutney

2 kg (4 lb 8 oz) ripe slipstone peaches
2 onions, thinly sliced
2 cloves garlic, crushed
375 g (13 oz/1²⁄₃ cups) sugar
600 ml (21 fl oz/2¹⁄₃ cups) cider vinegar
1 tablespoon yellow mustard seeds
2 cinnamon sticks
1 teaspoon ground ginger

Preheat oven to 210°C (415°F/Gas 6–7). Score a cross in the base of peaches, place them in a heatproof bowl and cover with boiling water. Leave for 30 seconds, then cover with cold water and peel the skin away from the cross. Cut the peaches in half and remove the stone.

Line 2–3 rectangular pans with baking paper. Place peaches in a single layer on the paper and roast for 30 minutes, or until they start to brown on the edges. (A lot of juice will come out of peaches.) Tip peaches and any juices into a large pan, and add onion, garlic, sugar, vinegar, mustard seeds, cinnamon sticks and ginger. Stir over heat until all the sugar has dissolved.

Return to the boil, then reduce the heat and simmer for 1¼–1½ hours, or until the chutney is thick and pulpy. Stir occasionally to break up the peaches and prevent the mixture from sticking to the bottom of the pan. Remove the cinnamon sticks.

Spoon immediately into clean, warm jars and seal. Turn the jars upside down for 2 minutes, then invert and leave to cool. Label and date. Leave for 1 month before opening to allow the flavours to fully develop. Store in a cool, dark place for up to 12 months. Refrigerate after opening for up to 6 weeks.

Red capsicum relish

1 kg (2 lb 4 oz) red capsicums (peppers)
375 ml (13 fl oz/1½ cups) red wine vinegar
2 teaspoons black mustard seeds
2 red onions, thinly sliced
4 cloves garlic, chopped
1 teaspoon grated fresh ginger
2 apples, peeled, cored and grated
1 teaspoon black peppercorns
230 g (8 oz/1 cup) firmly packed soft brown sugar

Remove the seeds and membranes and thinly slice the capsicums. Put in a large pan along with the vinegar, mustard seeds, onion, garlic, ginger and apple. Place the peppercorns on a square of muslin (cheesecloth), tie securely with string, and add to the pan. Simmer for 30 minutes, or until the capsicum is soft.

Add the sugar and stir over low heat, without boiling, until all sugar has dissolved. Bring to the boil, stirring often, then reduce the heat and simmer, for 1¼ hours, or until the relish is thick and pulpy. Discard the muslin (cheesecloth) bag.

Spoon immediately into clean, warm jars and seal. Turn the jars upside down for 2 minutes, then invert; cool. Label and date. Leave for 1 month before opening to allow the flavours to fully develop. Store in a cool, dark place for up to 12 months. Refrigerate after opening for up to 6 weeks.

Beetroot relish

750 g (1 lb 10 oz/5⅓ cups) fresh beetroot, peeled and coarsely
  grated
1 onion, chopped
400 g (14 oz) green apples, peeled, cored and chopped
410 ml (14 fl oz/1⅔ cups) white wine vinegar
95 g (3¼ oz/½ cup) lightly packed soft brown sugar
125 g (4½ oz/½ cup) sugar
2 tablespoons lemon juice

Place all the ingredients and 2 teaspoons salt in a large pan and stir over low heat, without boiling, until all the sugar has dissolved. Bring to the boil and boil, stirring often, for 20–30 minutes, or until the beetroot and onion are tender and the relish is reduced and thickened.

Spoon immediately into clean, warm jars, and seal. Turn the jars upside down for 2 minutes, then invert and leave to cool. Label and date. Leave for 1 month before opening to allow the flavours to fully develop. Store in a cool, dark place for up to 12 months. Refrigerate after opening for up to 6 weeks.

Spicy pumpkin chutney

1 kg (2 lb 4 oz/6½ cups) pumpkin, peeled and cut into small chunks
2 tablespoons oil
2 teaspoons cumin seeds
½ teaspoon ground cinnamon
½ teaspoon ground coriander
1 onion, chopped
2 cloves garlic, crushed
60 g (2¼ oz/½ cup) sultanas
80 g (2¾ oz/⅓ cup) firmly packed soft brown sugar
125 ml (4 fl oz/½ cup) malt vinegar
185 ml (6 fl oz/¾ cup) orange juice
1 tablespoon chopped fresh coriander (cilantro) leaves

Preheat the oven to 200°C (400°F/ Gas 6). Place the pumpkin in a baking dish and drizzle with the oil. Bake for 40 minutes.

Put the pumpkin and the remaining ingredients, except the coriander leaves, in a large pan. Add ½ teaspoon salt and bring to the boil. Reduce the heat and simmer for 10–15 minutes, stirring often, or until the mixture thickens.

Gently stir in coriander and remove from the heat. Spoon immediately into clean, warm jars and seal. Turn upside down for 2 minutes, then invert and leave to cool. Label and date. Leave for 1 month before opening to allow the flavours to fully develop. Store in a cool, dark place for up to 12 months. Refrigerate after opening for up to 6 weeks

NOTE: To get a thick and chunky mixture, use harder pumpkin varieties that take longer to cook, such as Queensland Blue or Jarrahdale.

Tomato and chilli relish

1 kg (2 lb 4 oz) tomatoes
500 g (1 lb 2 oz) cooking apples (about 3 apples), peeled, cored and
  grated
2 onions, chopped
1 teaspoon grated fresh ginger
4 cloves garlic, chopped
1–2 long red chillies, sliced
230 g (8½ oz/1 cup) firmly packed soft brown sugar
250 ml (9 fl oz/1 cup) cider vinegar

Cut a cross at the base of each tomato, place in a large bowl, cover with boiling water and leave for 30 seconds, or until the skins start to spilt. Transfer to a bowl of cold water. Peel away skin, roughly chop the tomatoes and place in a large pan.

Add the remaining ingredients to the pan and stir over low heat until sugar has dissolved. Bring to the boil,]reduce the heat and then simmer, stirring often, for 2–2¼ hours, or until the relish has reduced and thickened.

Spoon immediately into clean, warm jars, and seal. Turn the jars upside down for 2 minutes, then invert and leave to cool. Label and date. Leave for 1 month before opening to allow the flavours to fully develop. Store in a cool, dark place for up to 12 months. Refrigerate after opening for up to 6 weeks.

Pineapple chutney

1 kg (2 lb 4 oz) ripe pineapple
2 onions, chopped
½ teaspoon ground ginger
½ teaspoon ground cloves
1 teaspoon ground cinnamon
165 g (5¾ oz/¾ cup) firmly packed soft brown sugar
125 ml (1/2 cup) white wine vinegar
60 g (1/2 cup) raisins

Peel the pineapple and remove the tough eyes. Cut into quarters, remove and discard the hard centre core and dice the flesh. Combine with the onion, ginger, cloves, cinnamon, sugar, vinegar and raisins in a large pan and stir over low heat until all the sugar has dissolved.

Bring mixture to the boil, then reduce the heat and simmer for 1½ hours, stirring often, until the mixture has reduced and thickened and the pineapple is soft.

Spoon immediately into clean, warm jars, and seal. Turn the jars upside down for 2 minutes, then invert and leave to cool. Label and date. Leave for 1 month before opening to allow the flavours to fully develop. Store in a cool, dark place for up to 12 months. Refrigerate after opening for up to 6 weeks.

NOTE: The pineapple is ripe if it has a fragrant pineapple aroma and the central leaf pulls out easily.

Autumn chutney

500 g (1 lb 2 oz) firm pears, peeled, cored and chopped
500 g (1 lb 2 oz) green apples, peeled, cored and chopped
500 g (1 lb 2 oz/2½ cups) tomatoes, peeled and chopped
500 g (1 lb 2 oz/3 cups) onions, chopped
5 celery sticks, sliced
3 cloves garlic, thinly sliced
2 teaspoons grated fresh ginger
350 g (12 oz/3¾ cups) sultanas
1 litre (4 cups) white vinegar
2 teaspoons ground cinnamon
2 teaspoons ground ginger
460 g (1 lb/2 cups) lightly packed soft brown sugar

Combine all the ingredients, except the sugar, in a large pan. Bring to the boil, then reduce the heat and simmer for 45 minutes.

Add the sugar and stir until all the sugar has dissolved. Bring to the boil and cook for 30–35 minutes, stirring often, or until the chutney has reduced and thickened.

Spoon the chutney immediately into clean, warm jars and seal. Turn jars upside down for 2 minutes, invert and leave to cool. Label and date. Leave for 1 month before opening to allow the flavours to fully develop. Store in a cool, dark place for up to 12 months. Refrigerate after opening.

Peach and chilli chutney

4–6 medium red chillies
2 kg (4lb 8 oz) ripe slipstone peaches
500 ml (17 fl oz/2 cups) white wine vinegar
500 g (1 lb 4 oz/2⅓ cups) sugar
1 large onion, chopped
125 g (4½ oz/1 cup) sultanas
2 tablespoons grated fresh ginger
1 cinnamon stick
rind of 1 orange, cut into strips

Cut chillies in half lengthways, remove the seeds and finely chop the flesh. Wear latex or rubber gloves to protect your hands.

Cut a small cross in the base of the peaches. Immerse them in boiling water for 30 seconds, then drain and cool slightly. Peel off the skins, cut in half and remove the stones. Chop the flesh.

Combine all the ingredients in a large pan. Stir, without boiling, until sugar has dissolved. Bring to the boil, then reduce heat and simmer, for 1¼ hours, or until the chutney is thick and pulpy. Stir often during cooking to prevent the chutney from sticking or burning on the bottom, particularly towards the end of cooking time. Remove the cinnamon stick and orange rind.

Spoon immediately into clean, warm jars and seal. Turn the jars upside down for 2 minutes, then invert and leave to cool. Label and date. Leave for 1 month before opening to allow the flavours to fully develop. Store in a cool, dark place for up to 12 months. Refrigerate after opening.

Piccalilli

400 g (14 oz/3 cups) cauliflower,
   cut into florets
1 small cucumber, chopped
200 g (7 oz/1²⁄₃ cup) green
   beans, cut into 2 cm (¾ inch)
   lengths
1 onion, chopped
2 carrots, chopped
2 celery sticks, chopped
100 g (3½ oz) salt
250 g (9 oz/1 cup) sugar

1 tablespoon mustard powder
2 teaspoons ground turmeric
1 teaspoon ground ginger
1 fresh red chilli, seeded and
   finely chopped
1 litre (4 cups) white vinegar
200 g (7 oz) frozen broad
   beans, thawed, peeled
60 g (2¼ oz/⅓ cup) plain
   (all-purpose) flour

Combine the cauliflower, cucumber, beans, onion, carrot, celery and salt in a large
bowl. Add enough water to cover the vegetables, and top with a small upturned
plate to keep the vegetables submerged. Leave to soak overnight.

Drain the vegetables well and rinse under cold running water. Drain the vegetables
again. Combine vegetable mixture with the sugar, mustard, turmeric, ginger, chilli
and all but 185 ml (6 fl oz/¾ cup) of the vinegar in a large pan. Bring to the boil,
then reduce the heat and simmer for 3 minutes. Stir in broad beans. Remove any
scum from the surface with a skimmer or slotted spoon.

Blend the flour with the remaining vinegar and stir it into the vegetable mixture.
Stir until the mixture boils and thickens.

Spoon immediately into clean, warm jars and seal. Turn the jars upside down for
2 minutes, then invert. Label and date. Leave for 1 month before opening to allow
the flavours to develop. Store in a cool, dark place for up to 12 months. Refrigerate
after opening for up to 6 weeks.

Roasted tomato relish

2 kg (4 lb 8 oz) tomatoes, halved
310 g onions (11 oz), chopped (about 2 onions)
2 small red chillies, seeded and chopped
1 teaspoon paprika or Hungarian smoked paprika
350 ml (12 fl oz/1⅓ cups) white wine vinegar
340 g (12 oz/1½ cups) sugar
60 ml (2 fl oz/¼ cup) lemon juice
1 teaspoon grated lemon rind

Preheat the oven to 150°C (300°F/Gas 2). Line a baking tray with foil first, then baking paper. Place the tomato halves cut-side-up on the baking tray and cook for 1 hour. Sprinkle with the onion and cook for another hour.

Cool slightly, then remove the tomato skins and roughly chop. Place the tomato, onion, chilli, paprika, vinegar, sugar, lemon juice, lemon rind and 2 teaspoons salt into a large pan and stir until all the sugar has dissolved.

Bring to the boil, then reduce the heat and simmer for 45 minutes, or until relish is thick and pulpy. Stir often to prevent the relish from burning or sticking.

Spoon immediately into clean, warm jars and seal. Turn the jars upside down for 2 minutes, then invert and leave to cool. Label and date. Leave for 1 month before opening to allow the flavours to fully develop. Store in a cool, dark place for up to 12 months. Refrigerate after opening for up to 6 weeks.

NOTE: If available, Hungarian smoked paprika gives this relish a lovely smoky flavour. It is available at speciality spice shops and delicatessens.

Traditional chilli jam

8 large dried red chillies
2 whole heads of garlic
300 g (10½ oz) red Asian or French shallots
250 ml (9 fl oz/1 cup) peanut oil
100 g (3½ oz) small dried shrimps
1 teaspoon shrimp paste
120 g (4¼ oz) palm sugar, grated
3 tablespoons tamarind concentrate
2 teaspoons finely grated lime rind

Remove stems and seeds from the chillies and break into large pieces. Place in a bowl, cover with hot water and soak for 15 minutes. Divide the garlic into cloves. Peel and thinly slice the garlic and shallots. Drain the chilli and pat dry.

Heat half the oil in a wok over a medium–low heat and gently fry garlic, shallots and chilli, stirring often, until golden brown. Remove and drain on paper towels.

Place the shrimp in a spice mill, food processor or mortar and pestle and process or pound until fine. Add the shrimp paste, fried garlic, shallots and chilli, and process to a smooth paste.

Reheat wok and add remaining oil and paste mixture. Cook for 5 minutes, stirring, or until very aromatic. Stir in palm sugar, tamarind, lime rind, 1 teaspoon salt and 100 ml (3½ fl oz) water. Bring to the boil, stirring constantly, for 5–8 minutes, or until thickened. Spoon into clean, warm jars and seal. Store in a cool, dark place for 6–12 months. Refrigerate after opening for up to 6 weeks.

NOTE: This jam is thick and paste-like and will firm on cooling. Ingredients such as dried shrimps, shrimp paste, palm sugar and tamarind concentrate are available from Asian food stores.

Dried apricot chutney

500 g (1 lb 2 oz) dried apricots
1 large onion, chopped
3 cloves garlic, finely chopped
2 tablespoons grated fresh ginger
500 ml (17 fl oz/2 cups) cider vinegar
230 g (8 oz/1 cup) firmly packed soft brown sugar

125 g (4½ oz/1 cup) sultanas
2 teaspoons mustard seeds, crushed (see Note)
2 teaspoons coriander seeds, crushed
½ teaspoon ground cumin
80 ml (2½ fl oz/⅓ cup) orange juice
½ teaspoon grated orange rind

Put the apricots in a bowl, cover with 2 litres (8 cups) water and leave to soak for 2 hours. Drain and put 1 litre (4 cups) of the soaking water into a large pan. Make up with fresh water if there is not enough. Chop the apricots. Put apricots and all ingredients, except the orange juice and rind, into the pan. Add 1 teaspoon salt.

Stir the mixture over low heat for 5 minutes, or until all the sugar has dissolved. Bring to the boil, cover and boil for 45 minutes, or until thick and pulpy. Stir often, especially towards the end of the cooking time so the mixture does not stick and burn. Remove any scum during cooking with a skimmer or slotted spoon.

Stir in the orange juice and rind. Spoon immediately into clean, warm jars. Use a skewer to remove any air bubbles, then seal. Turn jars upside down for 2 minutes, then invert and leave to cool. Label and date. Leave for 1 month to allow flavours to fully develop. Store in a cool, dark place for up to 12 months. Refrigerate after opening for up to 6 weeks.

NOTE: Crushing the mustard and coriander seeds helps to release their aroma. You can use the back of a large, heavy knife to crush the seeds, or a mortar and pestle, or put them in a thick plastic bag and crush them with a rolling pin.

Sweet corn relish

1 green capsicum (pepper), seeded and finely chopped
1 red capsicum (pepper), seeded and finely chopped
3 x 420 g (14¾ oz) cans corn kernels, drained
1 tablespoon yellow mustard seeds, crushed (see Note)
2 teaspoons celery seeds, crushed
1 large onion, finely chopped
600 ml (21 fl oz/2⅓ cups) white wine or cider vinegar
2 tablespoons mustard powder
230 g (8½ oz/1 cup) firmly packed soft brown sugar
1 teaspoon ground turmeric
2 tablespoons cornflour (cornstarch)

Place all the ingredients, except the cornflour, in a large pan. Add 1 teaspoon salt and stir over low heat for 5 minutes, or until all the sugar has dissolved. Simmer for 50 minutes, stirring frequently.

Combine the cornflour with 2 tablespoons water. Add to pan and cook, stirring, for 2–3 minutes, or until the mixture boils and thickens.

Spoon immediately into clean, warm jars. Use a skewer to remove air bubbles and seal. Turn the jars upside down for 2 minutes, then invert and leave to cool. Label and date. Leave for 1 month before opening to allow the flavours to develop. Store in a cool, dark place for up to 12 months. Refrigerate after opening.

NOTE: Crush the mustard and celery seeds in a mortar and pestle.

Apple, date and pecan chutney

2 brown onions, chopped
1.2 kg (2 lb 11 oz) green apples, peeled, cored and chopped into
    small chunks
400 g (14 oz/2½ cups) dates, seeded and chopped
125 g (4½ oz/1 cup) pecans, chopped
2 teaspoons cumin seeds
2 teaspoons finely chopped fresh ginger
310 ml (10¾ fl oz/1¼ cups) white vinegar
125 g (4½ oz/ cup) sugar

Put the onion and 125 ml (4 fl oz/½ cup) water in a large pan. Bring to the boil, then reduce the heat and simmer, covered, for 10–15 minutes, or until onion is soft. Add the apple, and simmer, covered, for 15–20 minutes, or until the apple has softened. Stir often.

Add the dates, pecans, cumin seeds, ginger, vinegar, sugar, ½ teaspoon salt and 60 ml (2 fl oz/¼ cup) water. Stir over low heat for 5 minutes, or until all the sugar has dissolved, then simmer for 5 minutes, or until thick.

Spoon the chutney immediately into clean, warm jars. Use a skewer to remove any air bubbles, then seal. Turn upside down for 2 minutes, then invert and leave to cool. Label and date. Leave for 1 month before opening to allow the flavours to develop. Store in a cool, dark place for up to 12 months. Refrigerate after opening for up to 6 weeks. Serve with roast pork, ham, cold meats and cheese.

Sweet tomato and eggplant chutney

2 kg (4lb 8 oz) ripe tomatoes
500 g (1 lb 2 oz) brown onions, chopped
500 g (1 lb 2 oz) slender eggplant (aubergine), finely chopped
4 cloves garlic, finely chopped
2 teaspoons sweet paprika
2 teaspoons brown mustard seeds, crushed
500 g (1 lb 2 oz/2 cups) sugar
600 ml (21 fl oz) white vinegar

Score a cross in the base of each tomato and place 4–5 at a time in a heatproof bowl and cover with boiling water. Leave for 30 seconds then transfer to cold water and peel the skin away from cross. Roughly chop and place in a large pan.

Add remaining ingredients to the pan. Add 2 teaspoons salt and stir over low heat for 5 minutes, or until sugar has dissolved. Bring to the boil, then reduce the heat and simmer, for 50–60 minutes, or until the chutney is thick and pulpy. Stir often. Remove any scum that forms on the surface. Do not cook the mixture over high heat or liquid will evaporate too quickly and flavours won't have time to develop.

Transfer to a heatproof jug and immediately pour into clean, warm jars and seal. Turn jars upside down for 2 minutes, then invert and leave to cool. Label and date. Leave for 1 month before opening to allow the flavours to develop. Store in a cool, dark place for up to 12 months. Refrigerate after opening for up to 6 weeks. Serve with cold meats, steak, chicken or fish.

NOTE: To achieve the richest flavour, it is best to choose very ripe tomatoes for this recipe.

Mostarda di fruta

175 g (6 oz) glacé fruit
1 teaspoon cornflour (cornstarch)
315 ml (10¾ fl oz/1¼ cups) white wine
1 tablespoon honey
3 cloves
1 tablespoon yellow mustard seeds
¼ teaspoon ground nutmeg
½ teaspoon grated fresh ginger
2 cinnamon sticks, broken into pieces
1 tablespoon lemon juice

Using a pair of scissors, chop the fruit into even-sized pieces. Mix the cornflour with 1 teaspoon water and blend to a paste.

Place 200 ml (7 fl oz) water in a pan with the wine, honey, cloves, mustard seeds, nutmeg, ginger and cinnamon sticks. Bring to the boil, add the cornflour mixture and simmer for 5 minutes, or until the mixture thickens.

Add the glacé fruit and lemon juice, and simmer for 10–15 minutes, or until the fruit is soft and the mixture is thick. Spoon immediately into clean, warm jars and seal. Turn upside down for 2 minutes, then invert and leave to cool. Label and date. Store for a week before eating.

NOTE: Mostarda di fruta is eaten in Italy with cold meats, poultry and game. It has a very sweet flavour.

dried fruits

Dried fruits make a simple, yet delicious, snack to nibble on instead of crisps or lollies. You can also use crisp dried fruits, lightly dusted with icing sugar, (confectioners' sugar) as a garnish on a fruit mousse. Most fruits can be dried, except berries and those with a high water content. It is important to keep dried fruits cool and dry, otherwise they will discolour or go mouldy. They can be kept in an airtight container in a cool, dry place for up to 2 weeks.

Before you start the drying process, think about how you are going to slice the fruit to make it look its best. Apples, for example, are best sliced across the middle, while pears are best sliced lengthways. Fruit such as rhubarb can be shaped during the cooling process.

A mandolin is a hand-held slicer with extremely sharp, adjustable blades. Always use the safety shield when slicing. If you have one, a mandolin will make slicing some of the smaller fruit much easier. If you don't have a mandolin, you just need a good, sharp knife, so be careful! You can pick the fruit you wish to dry because of its shape, for example, star fruit. Adding lemon juice helps the fruit keep its colour, as does the sugar, but check your fruit regularly while it is drying to make sure it doesn't burn or get too brown. Cool any fruit thoroughly before storing it in an airtight container—it should keep for a few days before softening but can be quickly refreshed in the oven until it dries out again.

PINEAPPLE

Peel and remove the tough eyes from a medium-sized pineapple, then cut the flesh into 2 mm (⅛ inch) slices. Pat the slices dry with paper towels and spread them out on baking trays lined with baking paper. Sprinkle the pineapple slices lightly with sugar and cook in an oven at the lowest possible temperature for 3 hours. Turn the slices over approximately halfway through the cooking process. Check every now and then to make sure the pineapple pieces don't get too dark or burn. Remove the pineapple carefully from the baking trays when dry and cool completely before storing in an airtight container.

APPLES AND PEARS

Slice 2 apples and 2 pears as thinly as you can, about 2 mm (⅛ inch) thick, if possible, leaving the skin and core intact. Cut the apples through the middle to get a pretty star-shaped pattern from the core. Cut the pears through their length. Put both the apple and pear slices in a bowl, sprinkle them with a little lemon juice and toss to coat thoroughly. Pat the fruit slices dry with paper towels and spread out on baking trays lined with baking paper. Sprinkle the apple and pear slices lightly with sugar and cook in an oven at the lowest possible temperature for 2½–3 hours. Turn the slices over approximately halfway through the cooking process. Check every now and then to make sure the fruit pieces don't get too dark or burn. Remove the apple and pear slices carefully from the tray when dry and cool completely before storing in an airtight container.

STAR FRUIT

Cut 2 or 3 star fruit into 2 mm (⅛ inch) slices and sprinkle with the juice of half a lemon. Pat the star fruit slices dry with paper towels and spread out on baking trays lined with baking paper.

Sprinkle lightly with sugar and cook in an oven at the lowest possible temperature for 2–2½ hours. Turn the slices over approximately halfway through the cooking process. Check every now and then to make sure they don't get too dark or burn. Remove the star fruit carefully from the tray when dry and cool completely before storing in an airtight container.

RHUBARB

Remove the string and trim the ends from 2 or 3 rhubarb stems and slice into long, thin strips along the length of the fruit. Pat the rhubarb slices dry with paper towels and spread out on baking trays lined with baking paper. Sprinkle lightly with sugar. Cook in an oven at the lowest possible temperature for 2½–3 hours. Turn the slices over approximately halfway through the cooking process. Check every now and then to make sure the rhubarb pieces don't get too dark or burn. Remove the rhubarb carefully from the tray when dry and then cool completely before storing in an airtight container. If you want to be a little more creative, you can try wrapping the cooked rhubarb around the handle of a wooden spoon when cooling.

NOTE: To keep the fruit as crisp as possible, spread a thin layer of uncooked rice on the base of an airtight container, cover with baking paper and top with the fruit. The rice will absorb any excess moisture. Drying times may vary greatly, depending on the fruit chosen, the season and oven temperatures. Once opened, refrigerate for 1–2 weeks.

curds

Fruit curds are delicious spread on toast, scones, croissants or pikelets. They can also be used as fillings for sponge cakes, crêpes, tarts or meringues. If presented in decorated jars, they always make popular gifts, or pour into small jars, label, date and sell at your next school fête. The mixture of fruit and butter gives a rich, creamy consistency and taste which is hard to resist. They will keep for up to two months in the refrigerator—if they last that long!

LEMON CURD

Combine 1½ tablespoons finely grated lemon rind, 185 g (6 oz/ ¾ cup) soft unsalted butter, 185 ml (6 fl oz/¾ cup) lemon juice and 250 g (9 oz/1 cup) caster (superfine) sugar in a heatproof bowl. Place the bowl over a pan of gently simmering water, without touching the water, and stir the mixture until the butter has melted and all the sugar has dissolved. Add 12 egg yolks and stir constantly until the mixture thickens and coats the back of a spoon. This will take about 15–20 minutes—the heat must remain low or the mixture will curdle. Strain the mixture, reheat and then pour into clean, warm jars. Seal while hot, label and date. Keep in the refrigerator for up to 2 months. **MAKES ABOUT 600 ML (2½ CUPS)**

MANGO AND LIME CURD

Cut the cheeks from 2 large mangoes, cutting on either side of stone, peel and chop the flesh. Blend the flesh in a food processor or blender until smooth. Push through a fine sieve—you will need 315 ml (11 fl oz/1¼ cups) strained mango purée. Combine the purée with ½ teaspoon finely grated lime rind, 80 ml (2½ fl oz/⅓ cup) strained lime juice, 160 g (5½ oz/⅔ cup) soft unsalted butter, 250 g (9 oz/1 cup) sugar and 4 beaten eggs in a heat-proof bowl. Place the bowl over a pan of simmering water, without touching the water. Stir constantly until the butter has melted and the sugar has dissolved. Stir for 15–20 minutes, or until the mixture thickens and coats the back of a spoon. Remove from the heat, pour into clean, warm jars and seal while hot. Keep in refrigerator for up to 2 months. **MAKES ABOUT 875 ML (3½ CUPS)**

PASSIONFRUIT CURD

Beat 4 eggs and strain them into a heat-proof bowl. Stir in 185 g (6½ fl oz/¾ cup) caster (superfine) sugar, 80 ml (2½ fl oz/⅓ cup) lemon juice, 200 g (7 oz/¾ cup) soft butter, 125 g (4½ fl oz/½ cup) passionfruit pulp, and 3 teaspoons grated lemon rind. Place bowl over a pan of simmering water, without letting it touch the water, and stir until butter has melted and the sugar has dissolved. Stir constantly for 15–20 minutes, or until the mixture thickly coats the back of spoon. Spoon into clean, warm jars and seal while hot. Refrigerate when cool. Keep in the refrigerator for up to 2 months. **MAKES 600 ML (2½ CUPS)**

VANILLA BEAN AND LEMON CURD

Place 2 teaspoons grated lemon rind, 125 ml (4 fl oz/½ cup) lemon juice, 125 g (4½ oz/½ cup) soft unsalted butter and 185 g (6½ fl oz/¾ cup) vanilla-infused caster (superfine) sugar (see Note) in a pan. Stir over low heat until all the sugar has dissolved. Lightly beat

4 egg yolks and slowly drizzle into the lemon mixture while stirring. Return the mixture to the heat and cook over low heat, stirring constantly, for about 5 minutes, or until thickened. Pour into clean, warm jars and seal while hot. Keep in the refrigerator for up to 2 months. **MAKES 375 ML (1½ CUPS)**

NOTE: To make vanilla sugar, store a whole vanilla bean with the caster sugar in an airtight container for at least 1 week prior to use. Remove the vanilla bean before use. If washed and dried thoroughly, and stored in an airtight container, the vanilla bean can be reused three or four times.

STRAWBERRY CURD

Hull 250 g (9 oz) strawberries, chop roughly and put in pan with 185 g (6½ fl oz/¾ cup) caster (superfine) sugar, 125 g (4 oz/½ cup) soft unsalted butter, 1 tablespoon lemon juice and 1 teaspoon grated lemon rind. Stir over low heat until butter has melted and the sugar dissolved. Simmer gently for 5 minutes, then remove from heat. Lightly beat 4 egg yolks in a large bowl, then slowly drizzle into the strawberry mixture while stirring. The mixture will thicken as you add it. Return to low heat and then cook for 2 minutes while stirring. Do not allow to boil or the curd will separate. Pour into clean, warm jars and seal while hot. Keep in the refrigerator for up to 2 months. **MAKES 500 ML (2 CUPS)**

DRIED APRICOT CURD

Place 100 g (3½ oz/⅔ cup) finely chopped dried apricots in a bowl, cover with 125 ml (4 fl oz/½ cup) boiling water, and stand for 30 minutes. Stir to form a lumpy paste. Beat 4 eggs well and strain into a heatproof bowl, stir in 125 ml (4 fl oz/½ cup) lemon juice, 125 g (4½ fl oz/½ cup) caster (superfine) sugar, 180 g (6 oz/¾ cup) soft unsalted butter and the apricot paste. Place the bowl over a pan of simmering water, without touching the water. Stir until butter has melted and sugar dissolved. Stir constantly for about

15–20 minutes, or until mixture thickly coats the back of a spoon. Spoon into clean, warm jars and seal while hot. Keep in the refrigerator for up to 2 months.**MAKES 2½ CUPS (600 ML/20 FL OZ)**

microwave jams

These recipes are based on an 850 watt microwave. If your microwave wattage is different, cooking times may vary. Take extra care when cooking jams in a microwave, due to the extreme heat.

STRAWBERRY JAM

Put two small plates in the freezer. Hull and quarter 750 g
(1 lb 10 oz) fresh strawberries and place in a microwave-proof
bowl with 60 ml (2 fl oz/⅓ cup) lemon juice. Place the white pith
from 1 lemon onto a square of muslin (cheesecloth), tie securely
with string and place in bowl. Cook, uncovered, on high for
6 minutes, or until the mixture is soft and pulpy, stirring once or
twice. Cool slightly then measure. Add 250 g (9oz/1 cup) sugar
for every cup of fruit mixture and stir until sugar has dissolved.
Cook, uncovered, on high for 15–20 minutes, or until mixture
reaches setting point. Test for setting point during cooking (see
page 12). When jam is ready, discard bag. Carefully pour the very
hot (85°C/185°F) jam into clean, warm jars and seal. Turn the jars
upside down for 2 minutes, then invert and leave to cool. Label
and date. **MAKES 500 ML (2 CUPS)**

DRIED FIG JAM

Put two small plates in freezer. Remove the stalks from 500 g
(1 lb 2 oz) dried figs and place in a microwave-proof bowl with
375 ml (13 fl oz/1½ cups) water and 2 tablespoons lemon juice.
Place the white pith from 1 lemon onto a square of muslin
(cheesecloth), tie securely with string and place in bowl. Cook,
uncovered, on high for 10 minutes, or until mixture is soft and
pulpy, stirring once or twice. Cool slightly then measure. Add
250 g (9 oz/1 cup) sugar for every cup of fruit mixture and stir
until all the sugar has dissolved. Cook, uncovered, on high for
15–20 minutes, or until mixture reaches setting point. Test for
setting point a couple of times during cooking (see page 12).
Discard the bag. Carefully pour the very hot (85°C/185°F) jam
into clean, warm jars. Turn jars upside down for 2 minutes, then
invert and leave to cool. Label and date. **MAKES 1 LITRE (4 CUPS)**

CITRUS MARMALADE

Put two small plates in the freezer. Remove the rind from a grapefruit, a lemon and an orange. Remove the pith and roughly chop the flesh. Remove the seeds. Place pith and seeds onto a square of muslin (cheesecloth) and tie securely with string. Place the rind and the bag in a microwave-proof bowl and cover with 375 ml (13 fl oz/1½ cups) water. Cook, uncovered, on high for 10 minutes, or until rind is soft. Cool slightly, then measure. Add 250 g (9 oz/1 cup) sugar for every cup of the fruit mixture and stir until dissolved. Cook, uncovered, on high for 20–25 minutes, or until mixture reaches setting point. Test for setting point a couple of times during cooking (see page 12). Discard bag. Carefully pour the very hot (85°C/185°F) jam into clean, warm jars. Turn the jars upside down for 2 minutes, then invert and leave to cool. Label and date. **MAKES 500 ML (2 CUPS)**

APRICOT JAM

Put two small plates in the freezer. Halve and remove the stones from 500 g (1 lb 2 oz) fresh apricots and roughly chop. Place in a microwave-proof bowl with 2 tablespoons lemon juice. Place the white pith from 1 lemon onto a square of muslin (cheesecloth), tie securely with string and place in bowl. Cook, uncovered, on high for 6 minutes, stirring once or twice. Cool slightly, then measure. Add 250 g (9 oz/1 cup) sugar for every cup of fruit mixture and stir until all the sugar has dissolved. Cook, uncovered, on high for 15–20 minutes, or until the mixture reaches setting point. Test for setting point a couple of times during cooking (see page 12). If ready, discard the bag. Carefully pour the very hot (85°C/185°F) jam into clean, warm jars. Turn jars upside down for 2 minutes, then invert and leave to cool. Label and date. **MAKES 500 ML (2 CUPS)**

MIXED BERRY JAM

Put two small plates in the freezer. Place 500 g (1 lb 2 oz) mixed berries in a microwave-proof bowl with 60 ml (2 fl oz/¼ cup) lemon juice. Place the white pith from 1 lemon onto a square of muslin (cheesecloth), tie securely with string and place in bowl. Cook, uncovered, on high for 6 minutes or until the mixture is soft and pulpy, stirring once or twice. Cool slightly then measure. Add 250 g (9 oz/1 cup) sugar for every cup of fruit mixture and stir until all the sugar has dissolved. Cook, uncovered, on high for 15–20 minutes, or until the mixture reaches setting point. Test for setting point a couple of times during cooking (see page 12). If ready, discard the bag. Carefully pour the very hot (85°C/185°F) jam into clean, warm jars. Turn jars upside down for 2 minutes, then invert and leave to cool. Label and date. **MAKES 500 ML (2 CUPS)**

RASPBERRY JAM

Put two small plates in freezer. Place 500 g (1 lb 2 oz) raspberries in a microwave-proof bowl with 60 ml (2 fl oz/¼ cup) lemon juice. Place the white pith from 1 lemon onto a square of muslin (cheesecloth), tie securely with string and place in bowl. Cook, uncovered, on high for 6 minutes, or until mixture is soft and pulpy, stirring once or twice. Cool slightly and measure. Add 250 g (9 oz/1 cup) sugar for every cup of fruit mixture and stir until all the sugar has dissolved. Cook, uncovered, on high for 15–20 minutes, or until the mixture reaches setting point. Test for setting point a couple of times during cooking (see page 12). Discard the bag. Carefully pour the very hot (85°C/ 185°F) jam into clean, warm jars. Turn the jars upside down for 2 minutes, then invert and leave to cool. Label and date. **MAKES 500 ML (2 CUPS)**

liqueur fruits

Served over ice cream, with ricotta cheese or mascarpone, with brioche or panettone, or over toasted waffles or crêpes, these luscious, decadent liqueur fruits make an ideal finale to any meal. Make sure the fruit you use is just ripe and free of blemishes. Liqueur fruits should be left for a month before using to allow flavours to develop and must be refrigerated after opening.

APRICOTS IN RUM

Place 185 g (6½ oz/¾ cup) sugar in a pan with 500 ml (17 fl oz/ 2 cups) water. Stir over low heat until sugar has dissolved. Bring to the boil, add 500 g (1 lb 2 oz) dried apricots, reduce the heat and simmer for 3 minutes. Remove the pan from the heat and stir in 185 ml (6 fl oz/¾ cup) dark rum. Make sure the temperature is at least 85°C (185°F) and spoon into a clean, warm 1 litre (4 cup) jar. Seal while hot and leave to cool. Label and date. Leave for 1 month before using. Store in a cool, dry place for 6 months.
MAKES 1 LITRE (4 CUPS)

NOTE: It is very important to use a good-quality rum for this recipe as it will drastically affect the flavour.

PRUNES IN PORT

Place 125 ml (4 fl oz/½ cup) water, 90 g (3¼ oz/⅓ cup) sugar and 8 cloves into a large pan. Stir over low heat until the sugar has dissolved. Bring to the boil, then reduce the heat and simmer for 15 minutes. Add 600 g (1 lb 5 oz) pitted prunes, the thinly sliced rind of 1 orange and about 500 ml (17 fl oz/2 cups) port. Make sure the temperature is at least 85°C (185°F) and spoon into a

1 litre (4 cup) clean, warm jar. Seal while hot and leave to cool. Label and date. Leave for 1 month before using. Store in a cool, dry place for 6 months. **MAKES 1 LITRE (4 CUPS)**

NOTE: The prunes will swell during standing.

PRESERVED FIGS IN BRANDY
Place 750 g (1 lb 10 oz/3 cups) sugar in a pan along with 375 ml (13 fl oz/1½ cups) water. Stir over low heat until all the sugar has dissolved. Bring to the boil, then reduce heat, add 400 g (14 oz) firm fresh figs and simmer for 5 minutes, or until the figs begin to soften (this will depend on ripeness of the figs). Lift figs from the syrup with a slotted spoon, allowing as much syrup as possible to drain off and place them in clean, warm, wide-neck jars. Repeat with remaining figs. Gently shake jars to help settle the figs. Some syrup will accumulate in jars, so place the slotted spoon over the mouth of the jars and tip the excess syrup back into the pan. Bring syrup to the boil and boil for 10 minutes, or until it thickens. Remove from heat, allow any bubbles to subside and pour 375 ml (13 fl oz/1½ cups) into a large heatproof jug, reserving any remaining syrup. Stir in 375 ml (13 fl oz/1½ cups) brandy and pour into jars to cover the figs. If there is not enough brandy syrup to cover, combine small quantities of the reserved syrup and some of the brandy in a jug and cover figs. Make sure temperature is at least 85°C (185°F) and seal while hot. Label and store for 1 month before using. Store in a cool, dry place for 6 months. Refrigerate after opening. **MAKES 1 LITRE (4 CUPS)**

MUSCAT FRUITS
Place 150 g (5½ oz) prunes, 150 g (5½ oz) small dried figs, stems removed, 100 g (3½ oz) dried sliced apples, 100 g (3½ oz) dried peach halves, 100 g (3½ oz) dried apricot halves, 100 g (3½ oz)

raisins, 2 strips orange rind, 2 cinnamon sticks, halved, 4 whole cloves and 750 ml (26 floz/3 cups) clear apple juice in a large non-metallic bowl. Cover and soak overnight. Place in a large pan and bring to the boil, then reduce the heat and simmer for 5 minutes. Remove the pan from the heat and stir in 250 ml (9 fl oz/1 cup) liqueur muscat. Make sure the temperature is at least 85°C (185°F) and spoon fruit mixture and syrup into clean, warm, wide-neck jars. Seal, label and date. Leave for 1 month before using. Store in a cool, dark place for 6 months. **MAKES ABOUT 1.125 LITRES (4½ CUPS)**

PEACHES IN BRANDY
Place 6–8 (1 kg/2 lb 4 oz) firm ripe slipstone peaches in a large bowl, cover with boiling water and leave for 30 seconds. Remove peaches using a slotted spoon and refresh in a bowl of icy water. Remove skins, cut the peaches in half and gently twist and pull apart to remove stones. Place 250 ml (9 fl oz/1 cup) water and 125 g (4½ oz/½ cup) sugar in a large pan, and stir over low heat until all sugar has dissolved. Bring to the boil, add peach halves and simmer for 2–3 minutes. Remove the peaches with a slotted spoon and place into a 1 litre (4 cup) clean, warm jar. Add a split vanilla bean to the syrup and simmer for 5 minutes. Stir in 250 ml (9 fl oz/1 cup) brandy, then, making sure the temperature is at least 85°C (185°F), pour the syrup over the peaches, placing the vanilla bean inside the jar. Ensure that the fruit is fully covered with the syrup, leaving a very small space at the top of the jar. Seal and label. Leave for 2 weeks before using. Store in a cool, dry place for up to 6 months. **MAKES 1 LITRE (4 CUPS)**

fruit pastes

Fruit pastes are a delicious method for preserving an overabundance of fruit. They may take a while to cook, but they keep for well for up to a year because of their high concentration of sugar. They are delicious with coffee, as part of a cheese board or with cold meats.

QUINCE PASTE

Line a 28 x 18 cm (11 x 7 inch) tin with baking paper. Peel and core 2 kg (4 lb 8 oz) quinces, reserving cores. Cut into chunks and place in a large pan. Chop the cores, place on a square of muslin (cheesecloth), tie securely with string and add to pan along with 500 ml (17 fl oz/2 cups) water and 2 tablespoons lemon juice. Cook, covered, over low heat for 30–40 minutes, or until soft and tender. Cool slightly, squeeze any juices from bag and discard it. Purée fruit in a blender or food processor until smooth, then press through a fine sieve. Weigh purée and return it to the pan. Gradually add an equivalent measure of sugar (1 kg/2 lb 4 oz fruit purée = 1 kg/2 lb 4 oz sugar). Stir over low heat, without boiling, until sugar has dissolved. Cook, stirring with a wooden spoon to prevent from sticking and burning, for 45–60 minutes, or until the mixture leaves side of pan and is difficult to push wooden spoon through.

TO PACKAGE AND STORE THE PASTES:

Spread into the prepared tin and smooth with a palette knife. Cut the pastes into small squares, diamonds or triangles with a hot knife. Place a blanched or slivered almond in the centre of each piece or roll in caster sugar to coat, if desired. Wrap in foil and store in an airtight container in a cool, dry place. Disposable foil tins are ideal for storing fruit pastes. Spread the hot fruit mixture into them and press a piece of greaseproof paper onto the mixture before wrapping.

NOTE: As the mixture thickens, it will start to splatter. Make sure you use a large, deep-sided pan and wrap a tea towel around your hand while stirring.

APRICOT PASTE
Line a 28 x 18 cm (11 x 7 inch) tin with baking paper. Select 2 kg (4 lb 8 oz) apricots (you will need some to be a little green to help gel the paste). Remove stalks, stones and any blemishes. Cut the apricots into quarters and the remainder in half. Place in a large pan with 250 ml (9 fl oz/1 cup) water and 2 tablespoons lemon juice. Bring to the boil, then reduce the heat and simmer, covered, for 15–20 minutes, or until fruit is soft and tender. Cool slightly. Purée the fruit in a blender or food processor until smooth, then press through a fine sieve. Weigh the purée and return it to the pan. Gradually add an equivalent measure of sugar (1 kg/2 lb fruit purée = 1 kg/2 lb sugar). Stir over low heat, without boiling, until all sugar has dissolved. Cook, stirring with a wooden spoon to prevent sticking and burning, for 45–60 minutes, or until mixture leaves the side of the pan and it is difficult to push the wooden spoon through. (If the mixture starts to stick to the bottom of the pan, transfer to a heatproof bowl, clean the pan and return to the clean pan to continue cooking.)

PLUM PASTE
Line a 28 x 18 cm (11 x 7 inch) tin with baking paper. Select 1.5 kg (3 lb) plums (you will need some to be a little green to help gel the paste). Remove the stalks, stones and any blemishes, then cut into quarters. Place in a large pan with 250 ml (1 cup) water and 2 tablespoons lemon juice. Bring to the boil, then

reduce the heat and simmer, covered, for 20–30 minutes, or until fruit is soft and tender. Cool slightly. Purée the fruit in a blender or food processor until smooth, then press through a fine sieve. Weigh the purée and return it to the pan. Gradually add an equal measure of sugar (1 kg/2 lb fruit purée = 1 kg/2 lb sugar). Stir constantly over low heat, without boiling, until all the sugar has dissolved. Cook, stirring with a wooden spoon to prevent from sticking and burning, for 45–60 minutes, or until mixture leaves the side of pan and is hard to push the wooden spoon through. (If the mixture starts to stick to the bottom of the pan, transfer to a heatproof bowl, clean the pan and return the mixture to the clean pan to continue cooking.)

PEACH PASTE

Line a 28 x 18 cm (11 x 7 inch) tin with baking paper. Remove the stalks, blemishes and stones from 2 kg (4 lb 8 oz) peaches (you will need some to be a little green to help gel the paste). Cut each peach into 8 pieces and place in a large pan with 250 ml (9 fl oz/ 1 cup) water and 3 tablespoons lemon juice. Bring to the boil, reduce heat and simmer, covered, for 20–30 minutes, or until the fruit is soft and tender. Cool slightly. Pureé fruit in a blender or food processor until it is smooth, then press through a fine sieve. Weigh the purée and return it to the pan. Gradually add an equal measure of the sugar (1 kg/2 lb 4 oz fruit purée = 1 kg/2 lb 4 oz sugar) to the pan. Stir constantly over low heat, without boiling, until all sugar has dissolved. Cook, stirring with a wooden spoon to prevent from sticking and burning, for 45–60 minutes, or until the mixture leaves the side of the pan and it is difficult to push the wooden spoon through. (If the mixture starts to stick to the bottom of pan, transfer it to a heatproof bowl, clean the pan and return to the clean pan to continue cooking.)

heat processing

Make the most of the abundance of fruit available each season and preserve them to be enjoyed for up to a year later. They will keep for up to a week in the refrigerator, once opened.

Use either bottling jars with glass lids, spring clips and rubber seals, or Kilner bottles with metal lids and rubber seals. Ensure the bottles fit snugly into the pot and will be fully submerged in the simmering water.

TEN STEPS TO HEAT PROCESSING

1 Choose just ripe or slightly underripe fruit, without blemishes.

2 Thoroughly wash and dry the bottles.

3 Pack the fruit tightly to allow for shrinkage during processing.

4 Dip the rubber seals into boiling water to sterilize them before placing onto the bottles.

5 To make the sugar syrup, place the sugar and water in a pan. Stir over low heat until dissolved. Brush the sides of the pan with a wet pastry brush to remove any undissolved sugar. Bring to the boil, and boil for 3 minutes.

6 Cover the fruit with hot syrup (85°C/185°F). Tap the bottles while filling to remove any air bubbles.

7 Carefully close the lids.

8 Put a folded tea towel on the base of the stockpot. Fill the pot with warm water (38°C) to submerge the bottles.

9 Gradually bring the water to simmering (88–90°C), this may take 25–30 minutes, then simmer steadily for the processing time. Do not allow the water to boil. Check the water level regularly and top up with boiling water, if required.

10 When processing is complete, remove pot from the heat and remove some water. Wear rubber gloves or use tongs to remove the bottles. Do not put any pressure on lids. Place on a wooden board and cool overnight. Label and date.

To test that the seals on the spring-clip bottles are secure, release the clip and, with your fingertips, grip the rim of the lid and carefully lift the bottles. The seals will hold their own weight if properly processed. If they do not, store in the refrigerator and consume within 2 days.

PEARS
Mix 1 litre (4 cups) water with 1 teaspoon salt and 1 tablespoon lemon juice, or ½ teaspoon citric acid, in a large bowl. Peel 2.75 kg (5 lb 10 oz) Beurre Bosc pears, halve and remove cores. Place each pear in the lemon water mixture. Make a sugar syrup by dissolving 750 g (1 lb 10 oz/3 cups) sugar in 1.5 litres (6 cups) boiling water and 1½ teaspoons citric acid or 60 ml (2 fl oz/¼ cup) lemon juice. Arrange fruit in six 500 ml (17 fl oz/2 cup) bottles. Follow the 10 steps to heat processing. Cook for 30 minutes.

APRICOTS AND PLUMS

Score a cross in the base of 2.5 kg (5 lb 8 oz) apricots or 2.5 kg (5 lb 8 oz) plums. Place in a heatproof bowl and cover with boiling water. Leave for 30 seconds, then transfer to cold water. Peel away skins, halve and remove stones. Make a sugar syrup by dissolving 500 g (1 lb 2 oz/2 cups) sugar in 1 litre (4 cups) boiling water. Arrange fruit in six 500 ml (17 fl oz/2 cup) bottles. Follow the 10 steps to heat processing. Cook for 15 minutes.

PEACHES

Score a cross in the base of 2.5 kg (5 lb 8 oz) slipstone peaches. Place in a heatproof bowl and cover with boiling water. Leave for 30 seconds, then transfer to cold water. Remove skins, halve and remove stones. Cut into 1.5 cm (½ inch) slices. Make a sugar syrup by dissolving 375 g (13 oz/1½ cups) sugar in 1.125 litres (2 lb 8 oz/4½ cups) boiling water. Arrange the fruit in six 500 ml (17 fl oz/2 cup) bottles. Follow the 10 steps to heat processing. Cook for 15 minutes.

TOMATOES

Score a cross in the base of 2.5 kg (5 lb 8 oz) Roma tomatoes. Place in a heatproof bowl and cover with boiling water. Leave for 30 seconds then transfer to cold water and peel skin away. Make a brine of 4½ teaspoons salt , 1 tablespoon citric acid and 1.5 litres (6 cups) water. Stir to dissolve over low heat for 2–3 minutes. Arrange tomatoes in six 500 ml (17 fl oz/2 cup) bottles. Follow the 10 steps to heat processing, using the brine instead of sugar syrup. Cook for 20 minutes.

First published in 2010 by Murdoch Books Pty Limited

Murdoch Books Australia
Pier 8/9, 23 Hickson Road
Millers Point NSW 2000
Phone: +61 (0) 2 8220 2000
Fax: +61 (0) 2 8220 2558
www.murdochbooks.com.au

Murdoch Books UK Limited
Erico House, 6th Floor
93–99 Upper Richmond Road,
Putney, London SW15 2TG
Phone: +44 (0) 20 8785 5995
Fax: +44 (0) 20 8785 5985
www.murdochbooks.co.uk

Chief Executive: Juliet Rogers
Publishing Director: Kay Scarlett

Publisher: Lynn Lewis
Senior Designer: Heather Menzies
Design: Katy Wall
Editorial Coordinator: Liz Malcolm
Production: Joan Beal
Recipes developed by the Murdoch Books Test Kitchen

National Library of Australia Cataloguing-in-Publication entry
Title: Jams and preserves. Edition: Bitesize ed.
ISBN: 978-1-74266-018-9 (pbk.)
Notes: Includes index. Subjects: Jam. Condiments. Cookery.
Dewey Number: 641.852
A catalogue record for this book is also available from the British Library.

PRINTED IN CHINA

© Text, design and photography copyright Murdoch Books 2010. All rights reserved. No
part of this publication may be reproduced, stored in a retrieval system or transmitted
in any form or by any means, electronic, mechanical, photocopying, recording or
otherwise without the prior written permission of the publisher.

IMPORTANT: Those who might be at risk from the effects of salmonella poisoning (the
elderly, pregnant women, young children and those suffering from immune deficiency
diseases) should consult their doctor with any concerns about eating raw eggs.

CONVERSION GUIDE: You may find cooking times vary depending on the oven you are
using. For fan-forced ovens, as a general rule, set the oven temperature to 20°C (35°F)
lower than indicated in the recipe. We have used 20 ml (4 teaspoon) tablespoon measures.
If you are using a 15 ml (3 teaspoon) tablespoon, for most recipes the difference will not
be noticeable. However, for recipes using baking powder, gelatine, bicarbonate of soda
(baking soda), small amounts of flour and cornflour (cornstarch), add an extra teaspoon
for each tablespoon specified.